A Brand UW of Excellence

A Brand *UW* of Excellence

Reflections on Teaching and Learning

James K. Wangberg

Editor

A Brand of Excellence:
Reflections on Teaching and Learning

Published by the University of Wyoming
College of Agriculture
Laramie, Wyoming
www.uwyo.edu

ISBN 0-941570-31-2

Printed in the United States of America

To Our Students: The Reason We Are Here

Contents

Preface

The University of Wyoming published a book in 2000, *The Ellbogen Experience: Essays on Teaching by Award-Winning University of Wyoming Faculty*, edited by James Wangberg and Jane Nelson. It celebrated the twentieth anniversary of the university's highest teaching honor, the John P. Ellbogen Meritorious Classroom Teaching Award, and provided a "glimpse into the lives and practices of faculty recognized by peers and students for teaching quality." The inspiration for this publication, *A Brand of Excellence*, parallels that of *The Ellbogen Experience*, namely, the desire to recognize our outstanding teachers and give readers an opportunity to hear the voices of teaching faculty in the College of Agriculture.

Their collective voice is one of passion, dedication to teaching, caring for students, and a love of the profession. As you read these chapters, you will discover these and other common themes. Bracketing these themes are the opening and closing chapters, which may impress the reader for their unconventional and creative messages. Jeff Lockwood's chapter may surprise readers who do not know of his proclivity for going beyond the boundaries of his discipline and writing creative essays that span the sciences, arts, and humanities. For Lockwood, being an entomology professor was just an opening to a fuller academic experience in philosophy, just as his chapter is the opening to a book of colleagues' philosophies on teaching and learning.

In a similar way, Steven Horn provides the ideal ending to such a book with his personal literary style and reminiscences of college life, from his time as an undergraduate through a distinguished career as college dean and professor. The reader will appreciate Horn's writing and will not need much imagination to see how this scientist and academic finds passion in reading and writing novels and relating to the student experience, both his own and others'.

Sandwiched between these chapters are other diverse stories with common themes: listening to students, respect for students, recognizing different learning styles and contributions students can make, testing hypotheses and active learning, learning beyond the classroom setting, enthusiasm for one's subject and conveying it to others. Above all is a shared theme—the joy of our profession, each author finding pleasure in expressing it in very personal ways. No one expresses it in more personal terms than Rachel Watson in her heartfelt essay, "Listen for the Dune Buggies." Reading her chapter will offer every reader a glimpse into her classroom and knowledge as to why students sing her praises. Watson's recognition of the importance of listening to students and respecting what they bring to class are echoed by Raina Spence, Mary Kay Wardlaw, and Karen Cachevki Williams in their chapters. They also address the college's commitment to nontraditional students and diverse audiences such as extension educators' clientele. Spence shares the lessons one learns when teacher and learner are not only from different locales but also different generations. Wardlaw recalls the most amusing and effective interactions she has had with her extension audiences. Williams ties much of this together as she addresses learning as a lifelong process and one in which teacher and student share experiences and learn from each other, and listening is the key.

Further reinforcing these themes and others are chapters 2–5, which focus on ways of teaching and ways of knowing. Chris Bastian and Stephen Williams are evangelical in their commitment to a practical appreciation of the "dismal science," economics, and the importance of the hypothesis, or what Williams coins "organized doubt," in the sciences. Williams offers the reader a surprise ending to ensure one leaves, still doubting. Like Bastian, Wilson highly values the practical and hands-on approach to teaching and shares his personal tactics to trigger learning. Like so many of his co-authors, he underscores the importance of knowing your students and respecting their varied strengths. Reinforcing Wilson's tactics are an array of tales by Jolley, who, as only a parasitologist can do, tells stories from the crypt, what some might call "gross-out" stories of parasites and humans, stories not likely forgotten by his students—or this book's readers.

Settings for learning are emphasized in chapters by myself and Sonya Meyer, the first highlighting the special lessons learned through field trip experiences, and who would imagine that one of these lessons could come from a giant banana slug? Meyer convincingly makes the case for the unique opportunities in studies abroad, and of course has the international anecdotes to back up her proposition. It's clear from these two chapters, as with all the others, that each author has had experiences as both a student and faculty member that made lasting impressions with them and with others. They clearly love reliving such experiences in these essays.

A principal goal in initiating this book project was to give a voice to our teachers. The contributing authors not only represent a cross section of the college's academic departments, but they also represent a cross section of professional experience: early career, to midcareer, to late career, with age having nothing to do with their passion and energy.

I hope you enjoy reading the stories of teaching and learning that have meant the most to these special educators and, in doing so, gain an appreciation for the kinds of teachers and learners we have in the College of Agriculture.

—*James K. Wangberg*

Acknowledgments

I wish to acknowledge and offer my deepest appreciation to the members of the editorial board for their interest in and dedication to this project, and especially for their time and energy in reviewing chapter manuscripts and providing feedback to the authors. The editorial board included Deborah Healy Hammons, producer/writer for Wyoming Public Television and former UW trustee; Jane Varineau Nelson, director, Ellbogen Center for Teaching and Learning; Nancy A. Nichols, manager, Visual Communications; Robert S. Seville, associate dean, Outreach School; and Robert W. Waggener, editor, Office of Communications and Technology, College of Agriculture.

Special thanks go to Nancy Nichols for the detailed copy editing and for her expertise and support in all phases of the production and marketing process. We are also extremely grateful for Tana Stith's creative talent as graphic designer and for being part of the college collaboration in producing this book.

Obviously, this book would not have been possible without the enthusiastic response by our teaching faculty and educators, and their generous willingness to reflect on their careers and relate their experiences in these unique chapters on teaching and learning. I thank them first for their role as authors but foremost for their dedication to the university teaching mission.

1

Jeffrey A. Lockwood

Jeff Lockwood earned his Ph.D. in entomology from Louisiana State University. In his first sixteen years at the University of Wyoming, he authored more than one hundred scientific papers and received nearly $3 million to support his research on rangeland grasshoppers. Four years ago, he metamorphosed into a professor of natural sciences and humanities. He now teaches a workshop in nature writing, along with courses in environmental and natural resource ethics and the philosophy of ecology. He has published three collections of essays through Skinner House: *Grasshopper Dreaming: Reflections on Loving and Killing* (2002), *Prairie Soul: Finding Grace in the Earth Beneath My Feet* (2004), and *A Guest of the World: Meditations* (2006). Professor Lockwood's popular science/history book, *Locust: The Devastating Rise and Mysterious Disappearance of the Insect That Shaped the American Frontier* (Basic/Perseus, 2004), received critical acclaim. He has written for *Orion, Wild Earth, High Country News,* and *Quest.* Professor Lockwood's writings have been honored with both a Pushcart Prize from the most honored literary project in America and a John Burroughs Award for exceptional writing in the field of natural history. He serves on the board of the Rocky Mountain Land Library and the editorial board of the *Journal of Agricultural and Environmental Ethics.* He is currently working on a history of entomological warfare—how insects have been used as weapons of war, terror, and torture—with Oxford University Press.

What Really Counts

O Goddess! hear these tuneless numbers, wrung
　By sweet enforcement and remembrance dear,
And pardon that thy secrets should be sung
　Even into thine own soft-conchèd ear:
Surely I dreamt today, or did I see
　The wingèd Psyche with awaken'd eyes?

(from John Keats's "Ode to Psyche")

The American public has been warned that universities and colleges have fallen out of step with the mainstream, pursuing values that are radically divergent from those of the larger society. There are many reasons to worry about the state of the nation's institutions of higher education: dependence on corporate largesse, loss of credibility as an unbiased voice, shifting priorities from teaching to research (or, more precisely, overhead generation), bloated administrative structures, deteriorating physical plants, and compromised academic standards. Disjunction with the dominant culture, however, is not one of those reasons.

The University of Wyoming, as most educational institutions, faces many challenges—all of which, we are told, can be met with the same solution that Western civilization proposes for every other contemporary organizational problem. Every ill of our cities, schools, businesses, militaries, hospitals, and government agencies can be ameliorated with one drug—the universal palliative of the modern world: more.

The university's problems could be solved if only we had more. Our classes need more students, programs need more majors, departments need more faculty, faculty need more grants, administrators need more staff, athletes need more facilities, libraries need more books, and everyone needs more space, salary, and say-so. Surely this resonates with a society that would flourish if only it had more technology, more oil, more teachers, more computers, more doctors, more highways, more information, more consumers, more medicines, more profits, more growth, more

With permission of the publisher, portions of this essay are adapted from *A Guest of the World* (Skinner House, 2006).

jobs, more faith (or reason?), more security (and freedom), and—most of all—more mores.

Stories are one of the few things that nobody is suggesting we need more of. But here's a fable anyway.

> *Once upon a time, deep in the forest, there lived a community of rabbits. And, as happens with rabbits, it was not long before they had overpopulated their grassy glade. However, just across the stream was a sweeping meadow with patches of wild carrots.*
>
> *So the rabbits, not being dumb bunnies, thought they'd cross the stream. But being rather poor swimmers, they decided to build a raft out of fallen trees—which is quite an accomplishment given their furry paws and lack of tools. However, an industrious attitude can make up for natural deficiencies.*
>
> *On the big day, the rabbits shoved the raft into the creek, only to find that the water was too shallow to float the boat. Their ship was grounded, but their cleverness was undefeated. The rabbits put their furry heads together and decided to appeal to Mr. Beaver, who had a dam upstream.*
>
> *"Please, Mr. Beaver, tear down part of your dam so more water will flow into the creek," they begged, offering him access to the aspens in "their" meadow once they'd actually made the crossing.*
>
> *"Okay," sighed Mr. Beaver, being suspicious of the wisdom of rabbits. And he reluctantly proceeded to remove a few logs.*
>
> *The rabbits watched with delight as water poured over the dam. Having calculated that the flow of the creek would double (rabbits, being prodigiously fecund creatures, are very good at quantitative thinking), they rushed downstream to launch their raft.*
>
> *Again the rabbits shoved and pushed, forcing their craft over the cobbles. But, alas, the ship was grounded solidly as ever. Looking up from their labors, the rabbits saw the meadow on the other side slowly disappearing beneath the water.*
>
> *For although the stream had twice as much water, it had doubled in width but had grown no deeper.*

"How many this semester?" asked Richard, poking at a crouton.

"One hundred twenty," I replied, stabbing a mushroom. The salad bar was the best place to eat and commiserate on campus.

"That's not bad," he said, "I have a couple hundred students in sociology."

"You have my sympathy," I offered, "but the administration wants 'body counts.' And," I added, impaling a cherry tomato, "we're supposed to treat each student as an individual."

"Use the demographic gut-check," Richard offered.

"What's that?" I asked.

"Tell them that their parents were right. Each of them is unique and precious." He paused, munched on a sprig of cauliflower, then added, "Just like the other ten thousand students on campus."

That semester I devoted myself to learning more than a hundred names.

> *Six thousand thousand thousand centers bright,*
> *The galaxy of Man—each star's dark plight.*

The most difficult part of being a professor is telling students that they cannot be what they want to be. The reality of a future denied comes as a blow, but I owe my students both honesty and compassion. They deserve the truth, even if others have inculcated the great cultural lie: you can be anything you want to be. The truth is you cannot. But what if you could?

If I could be anything, then perhaps I'd be a major-league baseball player (a shortstop for the Dodgers, to be precise) or a Nobel laureate (either Peace or Literature, or maybe both if anything's possible). If I could be anything to which I devoted my mind and body, then the only reason for failure would be a lack of discipline, desire, and character. If I could be anything, then whatever I was would be a matter of whimsy. There would be no search for an authentic destination. Every outcome would be equally plausible. I would never feel called to anything, other than whatever venture satisfied a capricious urge. But I can't be anything. And that is good.

I can be many different things, and some ways of making my way in the world will surely be smoother than others. And I can change. But I am someone, not just anyone. I was born into a story crafted by evolution, society, family, and authors I have yet to know. This is not a script but a tale of where I've come from, a story that must be honored as I write my own chapter. Genetics assured that I would not be a world-class sprinter (bad knees); society assured that I would not be a headhunter (legal constraints); and family assured that I would not be a rabbi (Catholic upbringing).

We find it difficult to accept that we are limited in our journeys. But if there were no footprints behind and no path ahead, then we would wander aimlessly. We would be free to be anywhere but condemned to be perpetually nowhere. The liberal tradition yearns for unconditional freedom, but how valuable is a blank book into which anything may be written? If you could be anything, truly anything at all, then you could be me—or I could be you. We would be impulsively penciled characters, meandering through an incoherent plot, within a meaningless fable. Erased and rewritten at will, our stories would come from nowhere and matter to nobody.

The struggle of being human is to grope with one hand, feeling and probing the limits of our lives. And with the other hand, hold fast to another journeyer: an ancestor, a parent, a child, a friend, a spouse—or a teacher. A teacher who might go with us into the dark forest of self-doubt when we fear to step off a path that others have laid.

Most of my students who fail a course of study have had their route demarcated by others. Of course, parents and society provide a sense of direction, but the journey is not theirs. "Go west, young man," is very different guidance than, "Go to Laramie and become an engineer."

I persist in my duty, despite the emotional pain of denying passage to students. But their sadness is often mixed with relief, to which I can add hope. For with every difficult occasion of telling someone that a road is closed, comes the opportunity of unfolding a map revealing possibilities greater than the student had been led to imagine.

My students dutifully calculated the number of heartbeats per year and blinks in a lifetime. But the numbers weren't real to them. So, one morning I pulled out a box of graph paper with a fine grid—$1/25$ of an inch—and taped together a quilt of twenty-four sheets (the final one being precisely trimmed to 22,500 squares). "That's exactly a million," I declared to the class that afternoon. The students drew close enough to focus on a single square and then stepped back. "How many sheets would it take for the human population, if each square was a person?" one asked. "It would blanket a football field," I replied after a minute of extrapolation. They grew quiet, each envisioning a tiny square somewhere near the 50-yard line.

'Neath cloak of thought, the mind cannot conceive,
What naked eyes can readily perceive.

This summer, I'm on a personal crusade to save a dying practice. I am resuscitating the art of listening by following baseball on the radio. When I was a kid, I used to go to sleep in the summer while listening to the radio broadcast of the Triple-A Albuquerque Dukes. Having spent a fair number of evenings at the ballpark, I could picture the game as the play-by-play and color announcers narrated the story. Today our information is so intensely visual that authentic listening is a quaint anachronism. And this would be fine, except for one thing—we are still storytellers.

I'm encouraged by the surging sales of audiobooks, as this affirms our continuing passion for the spoken word. Some pundits decry these recordings as chipping away at our ability to read. They have good reason to be concerned, but there is a skill even more vital than literacy. Let us call it *listenacy*—the capacity to truly receive and deeply engage the human voice. Perhaps much of the world's injustice would be addressed if more people could read, but at least in the industrial nations, I wonder how many problems arise because we can't listen. Few conflicts have arisen because people failed to read the writings of one another; much blood has been shed because we failed to listen to what others were saying.

And this is why I'm discouraged by the growing fascination with "virtual courses" replete with spectral, online discussions. Sure, as a last resort for homebound students the Internet provides a kind of stilted dialogue that is better than intellectual isolation. But in my experience, these exchanges are rarely more than artless discourse. Perhaps I lack the technological sophistication or pedagogical savvy to realize the potential of electronic give-and-take through bursts of casually composed snippets. But this mode of communication seems ultimately devoid of a real conversation's subtleties of timing and pauses or an actual voice's nuances of tenor and volume (capitalized words with exclamation points are vapid substitutes for the range of intensity with which a voice can convey anger, outrage, confusion, surprise, or excitement). The subtleties of body language, eye contact, and hand gestures are lost in the disembodied world of e-mail. There is even a sense of the pornographic in these virtual relations, as we are unable to witness whatever pleasure or pain is experienced by a living, breathing human being. We know in a deep sense that to truly hear another person is an intimate act, joining speaker and listener. We take in the human voice and from it create a world that is an expression of two lives.

There is a good reason that I prefer to hear a baseball game on the radio than read the box score in the paper (of course, I'd prefer to be at the game with a friend, kibitzing, critiquing, and analyzing together). It is the reason ministers speak to us from the pulpit when we might just as well read their sermons, the same reason I tell my children I love them as they go to bed—when I could just write them a note and post it on the headboard. And when it comes to learning, a hodgepodge of students seated in mismatched chairs, crowded around a dilapidated table in a cramped seminar room has more virtues and fewer costs—in many senses—than an electronic chat room.

"Close your eyes," I asked. Two hundred lids quivered suspiciously. "Picture in your mind a football field." The exercise was safe and simple; their eyes shut.

"Now, cover the field in a tropical forest—imagine the dappled sun and the damp shade." I paused, then turned on the metronome. The rhythmic ticking was a bit slower than their hearts. "With each beat, your acre of forest disappears. That is what is happening today."

A couple of weeks later, a test question asked the rate of tropical deforestation. The previous year's class was given the number in a lecture, and about half of them got it right on the exam. This year's students only experienced the rate via the metronome; nearly 90 percent of them selected the correct value.

A number's mute. But I forever hear,
The scale of life that rings within my ear.

In math I was admonished to "show my work," and in English I had to turn in my rough drafts. As a student, these were annoying requirements—what difference did it make how I arrived at the correct algebraic solution or the well-crafted paragraph? Now that I'm a professor, I understand the value of seeing the labor that went into a final product. A colleague in engineering once told me that he didn't have any interest in such an approach because it smacked of making excuses: "In engineering there is no partial credit. You don't get paid half of a contract if you build a bridge that collapses under half of the specified load." Fair enough. There's something to be said for having standards.

But there's another reason for seeing a student's work, other than granting passing grades for failed outcomes. I know what went wrong. If I'm a good enough mentor, I can help the student avoid the error in the future. What's more, witnessing the struggle of my students has fostered compassion—not the sort of tenderheartedness that makes excuses for poor efforts but the kind that toughens my resolve as a teacher.

In my early days as a naive assistant professor, I told the students I'd match their efforts at learning with my own at teaching. I imagined their shortcomings were invariably due to a lack of self-discipline, a failure to devote themselves to scholarship. And often I was right. But in time I came to learn that when I was wrong, I was tragically wrong. I discovered that I shall never be able to match the blood, sweat, and tears shed by many of my students in their pursuit of learning and life.

I've come to know the schizophrenic pupil, who studied while his mind wrestled with insane thoughts muffled by psychotropic drugs. The sleepy-eyed student whose condition during my lecture was not due to a night of debauchery but to nursing a feverish child whom he had fathered and the mother had abandoned. The young woman arriving to my classroom out of breath and tardy not because she was irresponsible but because she'd been battling her way through a heart-pounding anxiety attack that left her gasping for air as she left her apartment. The student who escaped the suffocating smallness of her rural high school and fought the urge to drown her insecurities in alcohol while holding back tears of frustration with the problems I assigned. The young scholar whose agonizing abdominal pains (which doctors later diagnosed—after she dropped out of the university—as stemming from a rare intestinal disorder) left her contemplating suicide in the midst of reading for my course.

What if everyone showed their work? What if I knew how much struggle that custodian went through while relearning to walk after a stroke? Or how much angst went into the bookkeeper's having left her house without rechecking the door dozens of times to assuage the tyranny of an obsessive-compulsive disorder? Or how much gut-wrenching anxiety went into a co-worker's battle to begin his day without that pill, powder, or injection? I might appreciate slow and painstaking efforts, or overlook a mistyped purchase order, or wait patiently for a reply to an e-mail.

But I have to maintain some standard of performance and adhere to a minimal measure of quality—right? Or maybe, if I knew the labors of other lives, I'd apply that standard of performance to my own humanity and that measure of quality to my own soul.

⊷ ⊷

I've developed courses in "Natural Resource Ethics," "The Biodiversity Crisis," "Deep Ecology," and "Environmental Justice." I've engaged nearly four thousand students in such academic ventures. But I don't know if any student is leading a richer life, whether her work is more meaningful or his decisions more responsible for my efforts. When my sister began college, she was the sort of poorly motivated, unfocused student who frustrates me in the classroom. Not until she changed her major to nursing did her formidable potential and energy become realized. A few years ago, she was visiting a museum when a woman collapsed with a heart attack. My sister administered CPR until the ambulance arrived. I envy the certain knowledge that one has changed a single life.

> *To know one life is better for your own—*
> *Or hope to save a multitude unknown?*

Few events rivet a professor's attention in a college classroom. But here it was, the rare and wondrous occasion of a hand being thrust into the air—not with the tentative reluctance that suggests the student is offering an apology rather than an answer, but like some sort of martial arts exhibition. Even in the somewhat contrived conditions of our ongoing exercise, I took it as a silent endorsement of our effectiveness as a teaching team.

We should have suspected something was amiss with such an enthusiastic response to a question. Freshman students aren't normally so animated, even when they are certain of the answer and points are at stake. Booby traps can close with surprising speed.

Scott Shaw and I were team-teaching in the University of Wyoming's general education program. The challenges of engaging nonmajors in science led us to invent a game-show exercise in which students submitted questions extracted from the text. Then, we chose the ones that best illustrated important facts and principles. The exercise culminated with the students competing for points by answering the questions in class. Like the Monty Hall of biology, Scott pointed to the excited student, and the trap slammed shut.

"Six thousand years ago," he announced. Only a cursory glance of the figure on page 53 of E.O. Wilson's *Biodiversity* was necessary for one of his classmates to compose the question: When did the first humans appear on Earth? We'd heard stories of colleagues who had been goaded into impromptu creationism debates, but challenges by fundamentalist students were rarely so blatant. Perhaps we should have anticipated such a conflict, but there is no way to prepare a graceful parry of such a direct assault. He settled back in his seat, smugly awaiting a response. The other students shifted uneasily, like a crowd gathering with the first shove that foretells a schoolyard brawl.

Scott was emcee that morning, so ninety-two pairs of eyes turned to him. His options were limited. Ignoring the student was likely to provoke a more aggressive challenge. Confronting him was hardly a good idea, given that the student-teacher disparity assured little honor in victory. Another choice was to spend the balance of the period trying to salvage science on the student's terms. Anticipating that Scott would offer some form of a refutation, I prepared to play a supporting role.

"Right answer," he intoned dutifully. Ninety-three mouths fell open (mine included), and one sneer was animated with an arching of the eyebrows. I knew Scott was a staunch evolutionist with Catholic tendencies, although we hadn't discussed theology at any length. He was probably less tolerant of fundamentalism than I, but here he was giving away our credibility as scientists in two simple words.

But Scott wasn't quite done. The seconds of silence following his initial response had set minds reeling, and now he offered two words that put the world back into order. Offering an apologetic shrug and slight cock of his head, "Wrong class," he sighed disappointedly.

By Scott's adapting the essence of a Bible lesson, the class had been admonished to render unto religion what is rightfully spiritual and unto science what is material. A wave of palpable relief spread over the room. Gaping mouths lifted into knowing smiles, while one mouth opened in silent rebuttal. Set gently aside like a valued keepsake, the student searched desperately for a way to reconstitute the conflict. But a new batch of hands shot into the air, demanding our attention.

"This is insulting," she complained. My newly developed laboratory exercise on "big numbers" was not appreciated, at least by this student. However, experience showed that many of her classmates would not have mastered the difference between thousands, millions, and billions. This was quite a problem when lectures, readings, and problem sets made frequent reference to these quantities. Now I was facing a hostile business major who regarded my efforts to engage the class in an exploration of big numbers as a demeaning waste of her time. Scowling at the problem set, she grumbled, "I already know that a billion is a hundred times larger than a million." Perhaps the largest quantity true scholars can conceive is the magnitude of what they do not know.

No speed of Man can catch Perfection's soul,
To err but slowly is the scholar's goal.

Melody—one of the sweetest, kindest, gentlest women I've known—suffered terribly. Because of me. Her profound distress was difficult to watch, both because she was such a decent person and because I was the source of her angst. Melody was a student worker in the laboratory of my major professor while I was in graduate school, and she'd been assigned to assist me in my research. While engaged in the repetitive, mundane tasks that so often constitute science, we'd shared views of the world. And it was in this way that she came to discover that I'd not been saved.

As a devout Christian, she felt obligated to do everything in her power to bring others into the fold. But I was not just another heathen; I'd become a friend. So her sense of duty was even more compelling. She was very nearly desperate to keep me from walking into the fires of hell. And in my case, the impending spiritual disaster was made all the more tragic because I was not merely a lost soul—I'd consciously chosen the path to perdition.

Melody invited me to lunchtime Bible studies, which I gently declined. Finally, I felt so awful for her feeling so awful for me that I went along. But it was to no avail, like throwing a life preserver to a drowning man who refuses to grab the ring because he thought he was out for a pleasant swim. I know she prayed fervently for me, and I wished sincerely for her happiness. In the end she graduated and married a fine young man. So it seems that at least my wish was granted, although I suspect that she did not soon forget her drowning friend.

Perhaps my lingering memory of Melody stems from having been so often in her position in the years after I graduated. As a professor, I spent a great deal of energy trying to convert other people. There was the lazy-but-gifted sophomore whom I wanted to turn into a scholar, the arrogant senior I wanted to turn into a doubter, and the cynical graduate student I wanted to turn into an idealist. But they all, to a person, refused to reach out for my life preserver. Some even seemed happy while the pounding surf of mistaken perceptions and the crashing waves of unrealized potentials washed over them. I agonized over their fate and lamented their failings. I suffered for them.

At least I suffered until I finally realized that, while conversion was the appropriate intervention, I was trying to convert the wrong person. The essence of happiness lies not in changing students into people I can value and respect. Rather, the task is to turn myself into a person who can find worth and dignity in others. I'm still working on it. And so I still feel compelled to save others on occasion.

But at least now when I attempt a rescue, I don't stand on the deck of my ship and throw a flotation device. I jump in after them. Once there, I begin to understand that treading water on your own can be more appealing than wearing someone else's life jacket. Often what appeared to be drowning was truly a pleasant swim. And sometimes I find that being tossed by their waves is preferable to the navigational certainty aboard my ship.

— ⊷⊹⊶ —

With midterm exam scores averaging 67 percent, a radical detour in teaching seemed necessary to salvage the course. The class was devoted to the science of biodiversity, and I wanted the students to derive deeper meaning from the experience. Now, however, as I sat listening to each student's strained efforts, the idea of having them memorize and interpret poetry about the natural world seemed a failure. Until Eric—a rugged range-management major with a ragged series of quiz grades—sat down across the table, grew calm, and then serene. With genuine understanding in his eyes and passion in his voice, Eric recited the first poem (we learned later) that he'd ever committed to memory: "…To see a World in a Grain of Sand / And a Heaven in a Wild Flower, / Hold infinity in the palm of your hand / And Eternity in an hour…."

> *See a grain of sand or count 1, 2, 3…*
> *Does heart or mind bespeak infinity?*

I am a shaman. And I strongly recommend this practice because many of us have what it takes, and the world is in desperate need of shamans. I'm not referring to the entranced emissaries of the immaterial realm. Rather, I mean the living bridges between our sweaty, frantic lives and other grimy, chaotic worlds. You know: Jews who can speak with Arabs, liberals who can communicate with conservatives, chemists who can converse with poets, and aging feminists who can confabulate with teenage boys. I mean, modern shamans.

Traditional shamans live at the edge of a village, spanning the gap between human and nonhuman worlds. This physical location embodies their deeper purpose. As noted by the philosopher-anthropologist David Abrams, "The magician's intelligence is not encompassed within the society; its place is at the edge of the community, mediating between the human community and the beings upon which the village depends for its nourishment and sustenance." In the modern world, people find themselves abutting—and depending on—beings who seem every bit as unfathomable as panthers or poisonwood. Except that these other creatures are also humans.

For my part, I'm an academic shaman. Having the title of "professor of natural sciences and humanities," my task is to bridge the yawning gap between these ways of knowing. I afflict agriculture students with notions of human justice and animal welfare, and English students with contentions that one must know science to write well about nature. Creating dialogue within a university might seem rather mundane, somewhat beneath a genuine shaman. But the villages of the sciences and humanities have erected bulwarks of terms, techniques, and traditions, creating nearly impenetrable mysteries to one another. This would be fine, except the problems of the world are too urgent, education too important, and students too valuable for such provincialism. The sciences–humanities valley of academia is a microcosm of the portentous chasms to be spanned throughout the world.

Many a shadowy presence lurks in the twilight between our modern villages and the larger society. Ignorance is transformed into fear as we ascribe darkly malevolent intentions to those we do not comprehend. And there are few shamans to guide us, or at least few who have taken on this desperately needed role. We need compassionate and courageous guides who can teach us about them and let them know about us, so that our differences become a source of wonder rather than fear. Who will guide our students into the worlds of the homeless, the religious fundamentalist, the black, the learning disabled, or the schizophrenic? Do you know the world of war veterans, octogenarians, Muslims, AIDS victims, or inner-city youths? Can you show students the world of the paraplegic, atheist, ex-con, or drug addict? We need shamans if they are to understand, if they are to live as neighbors.

Abrams suggested that a shaman has "the ability to readily slip out of the perceptual boundaries that demarcate his or her particular culture... in order to make contact with, and learn from the other powers." Abrams was referring to natural powers, and we still have a great deal to learn from crows, forest fires, spring rains, locusts, apples, tsunamis, redwoods, and droughts. But as our village has grown, we no longer border only the natural world—as vital as it is to our nourishment and sustenance.

In the dusk we now see other forms, not with tails and branches but with turbans and burkas. Let us once again seek and heed the wisdom of the shamans.

Better yet, let us become shamans.

--- ◆ ---

The Endangered Species Act is daunting, but with guidance students comprehend habitat conservation plans, incidental take permits, and tradable development rights. However, at the core of the act lies a precept so alien to our economics, so foreign to our materialism, so strange to my students' world view that many are unable to internalize this simple principle. Despite my insistence that the Act places no limit on the worth of other life-forms, when asked on an exam what value the law places on a species of slug (an organism decidedly lacking in charisma), one-third of the students choose an answer that expresses the creature's worth in monetary terms. Refusing a million dollars for the last individual of a species is, for many people, inconceivable.

You can convert a Franc to Pound to Yen
If asked to price a kiss or laugh, what then?

There is perhaps no more universally accepted educational principle than: the ideal time to learn languages is while you are young. We might endlessly debate the best way to teach math, the definitive method for conveying grammar, the optimal means of engaging science, and the surest way to foster art, but when it comes to learning foreign languages, everyone agrees that the sooner one starts, the better. There is an exception to this rule, however. For there is a language so difficult to learn that one must mature even before making an attempt. And despite countless hours of drill, most people—including, and perhaps especially, university professors—fail to master it. We find it hard to be silent.

I had the requisite year of French in high school, three semesters of German in college, and in my travels I've temporarily grasped some useful phrases in Chinese, Portuguese, Russian, and Spanish. In other words, I've never come close to fluency. But I never struggled as mightily with these foreign languages as I have with my newest subject.

Silence is the most alien of tongues. Oddly enough, there is no difficulty of pronunciation, no challenges of grammar, no tricks of gender, no subtleties of tense, and no richness of vocabulary. The problem lies in actually putting it into practice. For silence is simple to apprehend but difficult to use.

Henry Adams claimed that he never labored so hard to learn a language as he did to hold his tongue. For more than forty years, I have argued, cajoled, debated, suggested, rebutted, ranted, pontificated, protested, and lectured. These forms of speech have often served me well in the classroom, but sometimes—maybe too often—they led to misunderstanding and confusion. With experience, I am learning that silence is sometimes more effective. Long moments of quiet allow students the time to think, to formulate questions, to construct responses, to ponder experiences, to gain perspective, to make connections, to learn. But the classroom is not the only setting in which being mute is well advised at times. Being a man of few words is especially appropriate when students come to my office with contrived excuses, rash accusations, impetuous complaints, unintended slurs, angry words, disingenuous flattery, and painful stories. And outside of my work, I've found that silence can be powerful and fitting while driving a long highway with a friend, walking a familiar path with a lover, gardening on a summer morning with a daughter, or fishing a mountain stream with a son.

As with any language, silence can be misinterpreted and misused. Saying nothing can be translated to mean that one does not care. An icy quiet can be a way of hurting those who seek our words. It must be said, however, that many of the problems that once appeared so enormous as to demand immediate airing with students, colleagues, or administrators crumble to insignificance with the perspective of a few quiet hours. I have often regretted rushing to speak but seldom rued waiting in silence.

I greatly admire my multilingual friends, but in middle age I've largely abandoned the dream of mastering French or German. I like to think that while learning new languages might be a gift of youth, wordlessness could be a grace of maturity—not unlike the difference between being smart and being wise. Knowing how and when to be quiet are demanding tasks. But with practice it may be possible to become fluent in silence.

In London, a hundred thousand; in New York City, fifty thousand—and in Laramie, seventeen people gathered at a park to protest the war in Iraq. The group included one of my students, who was asked by a local reporter, "What can so few people accomplish?" The young woman replied with a sweep of her arm. "There's nobody here but us," she offered. He cocked a graying eyebrow, and she went on. "Our voices are few, but they are infinitely louder than silence." He looked at her paternalistically. "We aren't here to be nice," she said tensely. "We came because it matters." He jotted a few notes and scurried to his car. The story never appeared in the paper. It would have been nice, but it didn't matter.

> *His chest expands: The arrogance of age,*
> *Proud winds are stilled: The breath of my young sage.*

2

Christopher T. Bastian

Chris Bastian is an assistant professor, Department of Agricultural and Applied Economics, at the University of Wyoming, where he received his B.S. in farm and ranch management and M.S. in agricultural economics. He received his Ph.D. in agricultural and resource economics from Colorado State University. Before receiving his Ph.D. and becoming a faculty member at UW in fall 2005, Bastian served as UW's agricultural marketing specialist from 1993 to 2005. He delivered extension education to agricultural producers in Wyoming and the West related to commodity marketing, integrated resource management, added-value agriculture, and risk management. He has received the Outstanding Extension Award from the American Agricultural Economics Association twice and three regional awards in extension from the Western Agricultural Economics Association. Bastian's current teaching responsibilities include agribusiness management, agricultural commodities and futures markets, and advanced agricultural marketing. His current scholarly activities focus on natural resource–based business economics.

A Funny Thing Happened on My Way to the Classroom:
What I Have Learned from Working with Producers and Teaching College Students

As a faculty member whose chosen field is agricultural economics, I am always a bit surprised when students resist learning economic theory. As someone who has spent years studying economic theory and being avid about its power to provide a useful framework for solving problems, I have become passionate about the importance of students grasping its major concepts. After all, if students understand the theory, they have a set of tools that can help them solve many of the agribusiness or natural-resource problems they may face in the future.

Unfortunately, students often do not share my passion for understanding theory, and they frequently resist theory-laden class material. This "theory stuff" doesn't seem too helpful to students. They want to get on with learning "something useful." After all, that is what they (or their parents) are paying for, isn't it, learning how to be better in agricultural business? Nevertheless, this "useless theory stuff" is the foundation of sound problem solving, and that is why I teach it.

My observation is students view theory as a waste of time because there doesn't seem to be a reward attached. Couple this student attitude with the typical graduate education experienced by new professors like me (hours of instruction dominated by theory), and you have the potential for disappointment by both the students and the instructor. The students provide less than flattering feedback on their evaluations, and the professor is left wondering why there seemed to be no appreciation for the hours of preparation that went into that semester's lectures.

How can college teachers overcome this dilemma and have an educational impact? I believe you have to motivate students to learn theory or course concepts through applications that provide a glimpse of the value in applying course content. This is a lesson driven home to me by years of providing extension education to agricultural producers outside the formal classroom.

The First Step in Being a Good Teacher

I still remember my first teaching evaluation. It was not flattering in many respects. Some of my very first thoughts (after dismissing a career change) included the following: "What is wrong with these students? Don't they understand how important this is? Don't they see how hard I worked to give them this great opportunity?"

After some serious consoling from a few of my colleagues, my thoughts eventually turned to: "What did I do wrong, and how can I do it better?" The point here is that a good portion of the burden often lies with the instructor when he or she gets that first bad teaching evaluation.

It is normal for anyone to try and teach someone else the same way in which he or she learned. After all, it worked for me, so it should work for them, too. Right? Maybe not.

My wife, who is a professional counselor, is fond of reminding me of two things relevant for this discussion. The first step in addressing a problem is admitting you have one, and the second step is acknowledging that not everyone is like you.

I often jokingly tell my colleagues that "once you get a Ph.D., you are admitting to the world you are a geek." I admit it. I have an agricultural economics affliction. The fact is I think this economic theory stuff is great, and what's more, I can't understand why everyone doesn't want to sit through hours of graphs and math to understand all its wonderful detail!

Despite my serious passion for agricultural economics, I now realize, as painful as it is to admit, not everyone learns economic theory like me through wonderfully drawn graphs or mathematical equations. So I have tried to become a better teacher after attending the school of hard knocks.

My Observations of College and Extension Students

Several years after completing my master's degree, I found myself faced with an opportunity to help agricultural producers. I seized the opportunity and, ultimately, was fortunate enough to spend nearly twelve years delivering extension education to producers in Wyoming and the West. The subjects I dealt with as UW agricultural marketing specialist included commodity marketing, risk management, value-added agriculture, and integrated resource management. During that time I also taught an agricultural commodities and futures course offered here in the Department of Agricultural Economics when there was no one else to teach it. Over time I found more and more of the lessons I learned from my extension experience (and ultimately extension material I developed) influencing my classroom approach.

Extension Students

Students attending my extension classes were largely agricultural producers. They came to the noncredit extension classes voluntarily, often to improve their business. Their desire to do better in business meant they were motivated by a strong desire for a better livelihood or lifestyle. Moreover, extension classes were usually offered during a time of the year and day that was designed to work with producers' operations. This usually meant extension sessions were short and involved only one meeting between instructor and producers.

Given the brevity of the session, I did not have the luxury to develop a theoretical foundation before showing how the concept could be used to solve problems. To have an impact, I had to make sure producers saw the potential benefit of the education very quickly, or I found myself talking to an empty room after the coffee or bathroom break. This meant jumping into an example, hands-on problem, or exercise applying the concept quickly, or I literally would lose my students!

College Students

I have found that college students attend lectures for different reasons than agricultural producers. The typical college student attends class so he or she can work toward a degree. Generally this overall goal motivates students to come to class. Ultimately students in class range from being very interested in the topic to only being there to meet a degree requirement. This often means students in the classroom require more motivation from the instructor about the usefulness of the subject. The college students need to see how knowing the lecture material is useful or may benefit them.

Another important difference between the college classroom and the extension class is time. As mentioned previously, the typical extension class is a short, one-time contact, but the typical college course is offered over multiple classes, allowing more time to teach a concept. This lack of time constraint and need for immediate payoff creates the illusion that I can spend more time teaching theory before talking about how it can be used to solve a problem. The problem with this illusion is the discussion of the application can sometimes be cut short.

When I was a student, I sat through many lectures that spent a lot of time elegantly explaining theory without ever discussing a potential real-world application. This usually happened in my non-ag courses. For me this was like sitting down to a meal and never getting to eat the main course. It only partially satisfied my hunger. I can only imagine how a student mildly interested in a subject feels with this approach or how a producer might feel spending his or her precious time only to be left without something concrete to take away from the session.

These observations have shaped my belief that a teacher needs to illustrate the application, or get to the "meat and potatoes," in a timely manner, if he or she is to have an educational impact. I believe this is true whether traditional college students or producers are sitting in the seats in front of me. Interestingly, much education research points to the same conclusion.

What Do Experts Say About Agricultural Students and How They Learn?

Do the experts agree with my assessment? A number of theories have been developed and research conducted about student learning styles. They largely suggest teaching theory through application. One area of research relating to this notion deals with psychological or personality traits and learning styles.

Katharine Briggs and her daughter, Isabel Briggs Myers, created a tool using Carl Jung's (1971) theory on psychological types to indicate personality types (Briggs and Myers 1988). This tool measures people's tendencies or preferences regarding how they relate to their surroundings. Using a simple test, the Myers-Briggs Type Indicator (MBTI) shows whether you are extroverted or introverted, sensing or intuitive, thinking or feeling, and judging or perceiving. If you are extroverted, you relate more easily to people and things, and if you are introverted, you tend to relate more easily to concepts and ideas. If you are someone who forms perceptions through sensing, you like working with facts, direct information from the five senses, and focusing on immediate awareness, but if you are more intuitive, you like to focus on possibilities, meanings, and relationships via insight. If you are someone who prefers to make decisions via thinking, you base your decisions on logical analysis. If, on the other hand, you prefer to make decisions via feeling, you tend to make decisions based on values. If you are someone who prefers judging, you like a planned and ordered way of life. Those who prefer perceiving like a flexible, spontaneous way of life. A score for the MBTI can measure how people orient themselves to the world around them and consequently how they learn new things, which has become important information for college professors.

C. Schroeder (1993) gave the MBTI to fifteen years of incoming college students and found that approximately 60 percent of entering students had a "practical" rather than a "theoretical" orientation toward learning, and the research indicated that percentage was growing. Those results suggest that active modes of teaching and learning are the most effective with current students; hence, using only math and graphs probably doesn't work well with many of today's students.

Research on people attending extension programs indicated something similar. J.T. Horner and L.A. Barrett (1987) gave farm couples attending extension farm management programs the MBTI to find out how they might make business decisions and use extension information. They found that the largest percentage of men attending the programs (25.3 percent) had an introverted, sensing, thinking, and judgmental personality type, whereas the largest percentage of women (17.8 percent) were introverted, sensing, feeling, and judgmental (the only difference being that women were more feeling in forming their perceptions). Initially you might think that introverted agricultural producers would prefer to learn different management strategies through self-directed study, but given the other elements of their preferences this might not be the case. Randolph Weigel (1999), at the University of Wyoming, suggests producers in these categories deal best with management situations through accumulation of experience.

New strategies in which they have no experience can be confusing to them. Again, this points to using examples and providing plenty of experiences to students in agricultural classrooms (college or extension).

R. Dunn and K. Dunn (1993) worked with secondary students in grades 7 through 12 and concluded that learning styles were affected by things such as physical environment, emotionality, sociological factors, and physiological factors, including perceptual preferences. This means some people prefer to learn in a team setting, alone or in a pair. Perceptual style relates to how students like to learn new things. Do they like to learn new material by listening (auditory), seeing (visual), touching (tactile), or doing (kinesthetic)? J.E. Brooks-Harris and S.R. Stock-Ward (1999) recommend assessing these different preferences and creating an environment in the classroom that matches the students. Again, all this seems to mean that a boring lecture of math and graphs won't likely appeal to a number of students' learning preferences. A mix of talking, drawing, examples, and activities will reach the widest range of students.

As I get older, I sound more like my father when I talk about the younger generation. I remember hearing, "What are these young kids thinking nowadays?" Well, some researchers have asked this very question. A number of college students are part of a generation termed Generation X, young adults born between 1961 and 1981 (Coupland 1991). They are the first generation in our history to grow up with the average household having both parents working outside the home. Being left at home after school has made these Xers more self-reliant and independent problem solvers. Moreover they typically grew up using personal computers (Caudron 1997). According to S. Caudron's research (1997), Xers have been conditioned to expect immediate gratification, and, thus, they expect immediate answers and quick feedback. This means today's students want to see the usefulness of information sooner rather than later.

P. Scott and J. Zebrowski (1998) say that professors from an older generation like the baby boomers are likely not teaching the way Xers prefer to learn. Xers consider college to be a means to get a job, and thus they have action-oriented learning preferences with an emphasis on results. That seems to fit with what I have been saying. Right?

Unfortunately I learned from baby-boom teachers, and what they prefer to focus on is process, typically finding multiple tasks and technology to be distracting (Scott and Zebrowski 1998). Again, that suggests my graduate education experience does not reflect today's students' learning preferences.

Jill Bale and Donna Dudney, associate professor and assistant professor of finance, respectively, conducted a survey of students at five universities to see if they could learn how to better teach finance to traditional-aged, Generation X college students (Bale and Dudney 2000). Their survey focused on two theories related to learning style. One model, or style, called *andragogy* assumes that learners prefer to be self-directed, and a key function of the educator is to determine how to meet the learner's needs. This is usually thought to relate to adult learning. Professors teaching such learners should encourage and nurture the transformation from dependency to self-directed learning. Students who prefer the pedagogical model or style prefer to passively receive knowledge. This means educators completely determine course direction, course objectives, relevant topics, and evaluation methods with these students. The survey results indicated most traditional-aged college students preferred andragogical learning, with the exception of being dependent on the educator for course direction (pedagogical trait). Foreign students who took the survey preferred pedagogical teaching methods, however. Professors Bale and Dudney recommended a hybrid method of teaching that applies andragogical and pedagogical theories, that is, directing students but also allowing them to actively learn things on their own.

J. Patrick McCarthy and Liam Anderson (2000) compared answers to test questions in history and political science courses from students who had active-learning activities in class versus those who didn't. They concluded that students who participated in role-plays and collaborative exercises (active-learning activities) did better on standard exam questions than students receiving traditional lectures. Noel Capon and Deanna Kuhn (2004), from Columbia University, conducted an experiment regarding student learning of two concepts taught in different ways. For one part of the experiment, students were taught one concept through problems while the other concept was taught through traditional lectures. In another class, the first concept was taught using lecture while Concept 2 was taught using a problem-based format. The professors then used two different forms of learning assessment at six and twelve weeks after instruction.

At the initial assessment, the lecture-discussion group showed superior learning for the first concept, and both groups performed equally well regarding the second concept. At the later assessment, however, the two different groups performed the same for each of the concepts. However, each group of students showed superior ability to explain the concept they learned through a problem-based format. The professors concluded that problem-based learning increases understanding of the concept but not necessarily a student's ability to recall a concept. Both of the experiments point to active learning through problems or activities as having more educational impact.

John Ricketts, Frederick Rohs, and Garvie Nichols (2005) surveyed one hundred students attending Abraham Baldwin Agricultural College regarding their learning styles and preferences. They based the survey questions on the Experiential Learning Theory developed by D.A. Kolb (1984). Kolb believes learning is a four-stage process, which includes learners having experiences, reflecting on them, deducing generalizations about the experience, and then using them as a guide to further action. Stage 1, "concrete experience," emphasizes feeling as opposed to thinking and an intuitive approach to problem solving as opposed to a systematic, scientific approach to problem solving. Stage 2, "reflective observation," focuses on understanding meanings of ideas by observing and describing them. Stage 3, "abstract conceptualization," is a conceptual, analytically based approach to learning. People in this category focus on logic, ideas, precision, and concepts, emphasizing thinking and analyzing ideas. Stage 4, "active experimentation," is an action-based approach to learning. This involves practical applications, looking for what works, and doing, as opposed to reflective understanding and observation.

The results of the survey indicated that across all majors, "active experimentation" was the number one learning method. "Reflective observation" was a distant second. "Abstract conceptualization" and "concrete experience" were the least prominent learning methods. The researchers concluded that faculty at agricultural colleges must incorporate real-world, hands-on applications into their courses.

The overwhelming conclusion drawn from these experts' results is that most students probably don't learn the way I do, and theory communicated primarily in lecture through graphs and/or math probably isn't going to create a passion for economics from most of my students. Hence, the lecture that I spent so much time to carefully prepare and deliver during my first stint in the classroom resulted in disappointing teaching evaluations. And research points to why this was the case.

While I hadn't done the research to know this probable difference in learning styles at the time, that first evaluation affected me and led to a new approach to teaching in and out of the classroom after that. I began teaching all students more like producers attending extension programs.

What I Have Learned About Teaching

My experiences in and out of the classroom have taught me that both producers and traditional college students need to understand how theory can be applied to solve real-world problems. The experts seem to agree that using applications, or problem-based teaching, is better than plain old lectures. Given this observation, my classroom teaching has evolved to be much more like my extension teaching. I do my best to give plenty of examples and provide experiential activities designed to show students the power of theory and concepts covered in class via application in realistic settings. This is how I have tried to reach a balance between theory and application. It is reassuring to me that this approach, based on conclusions drawn years ago from my experiences, seems to be substantiated by the experts doing research in this area. I literally stumbled onto this over time. I am reminded of a saying I often heard when growing up: "Son, even a blind sow finds an acorn once in a while!"

Examples of Realistic Experiential Activities

Now that I have laid a foundation for why I believe application through experiential activities is important, how does one make that work?

There has to be some boring old lecture before jumping into the activity, or the students just learn by trial and error. Basically, I try to lecture and give examples in class coupled with homework. I also assign students major experiential activities or projects that allow students to learn by doing. Thus, we are now at the stage where some examples of experiential activities and student feedback are needed to illustrate the merits of this approach.

I will focus on two simulations that I have used in both extension and the classroom. The first simulation sets students up with a farm or ranch business and forces them to make decisions in the face of different agricultural business risks. The risks and the consequences are based on real-world data and allow students to apply risk management concepts. Risk management here means to make business decisions that reduce the likelihood of having a bad business outcome due to something out of the business's control, like weather or a volatile market. The second simulation forces students to make commodity marketing decisions using different tools discussed in class during a real live market. The students have to market cattle, corn, and wheat and try to make the most money possible.

Risk Management

Before jumping into the details of the risk management simulation, I will give some background so we understand why risk management may be an important skill for agricultural businesses. The mid-1990s dramatically changed the business environment that agricultural producers face. International trade agreements such as GATT (General Agreement on Tariffs and Trade) and NAFTA (North American Free Trade Agreement) removed trade barriers and greatly increased the volatility in agricultural product markets. The 1996 FAIR Act (Food, Agriculture Improvement Reform Act) tried to reduce commodity program payments being dependent on agricultural production requirements. Additionally, the FAIR Act mandated that risk management education be provided to agriculturalists. During the tenure of the 1996 act, commodity supplies in the United States increased and commodity prices generally decreased. Although the latest farm bill has continued payment programs to producers in an effort to address lower agricultural incomes, the market environment remains much riskier than it was prior to the mid-1990s. Risk management education continues to be a priority in and out of the classroom to improve agribusiness managers' risk management skills. As a former extension educator, I spent a fair amount of my time and grant dollars working with my colleagues around the West to educate producers about risk management.

The typical agricultural economics program related to risk management focuses on approaches to reduce income volatility in the business by making different production decisions or using different marketing methods. Another tool available to producers is crop insurance. Analyzing financial statements and making better financial decisions, and/or reducing legal costs by addressing potential risks and liabilities, are also important risk management strategies. As you can imagine, a number of difficult concepts are dealt with in risk management education. These concepts may include assessing trade-offs between the risk of a management strategy and how much money can be made, different commodity marketing tools, analyzing financial statements, and legal liability of different alternatives. All of these topics also have underlying theories that are important for decision making.

How do you make the subject of risk management interesting to producers or college students without overwhelming or losing them? Toward the end of my tenure as an extension educator, I was fortunate enough to work with a group of educators in the West who developed a computerized simulation to help teach risk management. This simulation utilizes real-world probabilities of different market and production outcomes with different farming and ranching scenarios. Students are given the case ranch or farm and forced to make management decisions and see the potential consequences, in terms of income and amount produced, of those decisions (see www.rightrisk.org for more information on the simulations used).

The normal extension class using this simulation lasts about two hours. During that time, producers/students receive information on the basic sources of risk (production, market, financial, legal, and human) and potential management strategies. An example is given that illustrates risks and returns from different weather events (bad, normal, and mild winter) and management decisions related to buying or selling hay in those cases. The take-home message from this part of the presentation is that producers can only control their management decisions, not the weather. The students are then broken into management teams and given their farm or ranch (a laptop with the simulation loaded and ready to go). A prize is offered to the management team that makes the most money after eight quarters of play. The extension educators facilitate the simulation by walking the management teams through the first year (which usually involves taking no risk management action) along with the other management teams. The management teams are then allowed to play the last year on their own while asking questions of the educators as necessary.

Keep in mind the scenarios used in the simulation are based on real-world data associated with costs, production, and probabilities of potential events happening. During each quarter, different risks and management decisions could be made. Each screen provides information about the chances of something occurring and the potential consequences of the decisions. For example, one risk includes the potential for a bad, normal, or mild winter, and management teams could make a decision to purchase, sell, or keep the same amount of hay they currently had stored going into the winter feeding period. If they didn't have enough hay and a bad winter occurred (the computer randomly assigns winter conditions), the simulation purchases hay at a higher price and more calves die compared to a normal winter. During the simulation itself, the extension students ask questions of the educators, talking about the decisions they had to make and discussing what they would do on their own place if they faced this. In short, there is a lot of hands-on, active learning taking place.

After all of the management teams finish playing the simulation, the educators give a prize to the team that made the most money. The students are then asked, "Were you good managers or were you just lucky?" This opens up the door to discussion about management strategies in the face of risk and potential tradeoffs between reducing risk and income. The educators then have the management teams enter a screen where the computer can replay all of their management decisions over a 100-year period. After this long-run simulation of each team's management decisions, a screen showing how often, the high and low, and variability of income over the 100 years is displayed. The discussion then focused on different measures of risk reduction, and prizes are given to the teams that had the least variability in income and the least number of negative-income years. A number of concepts related to risk management are discussed via this simulation in a short two-hour educational session.

The question becomes whether this approach appeals to students and ultimately has an educational impact. The evaluations for this type of risk management workshop received some of the highest ratings I received as an extension educator. Comments about what students liked the best regarding the educational session included the following: "Straightforward—easily understood." "All of it." "The computer game made application very acceptable and interesting." "How interesting you have made a usually dry, boring subject—good investment of time." "Hands-on—challenges you to consider your personal style." While these comments do not prove this approach had a long-term impact, they do suggest students were interested in the topic, enjoyed the presentation, and liked the application. It seems more likely students would remember concepts from this type of session than a lecture on such a "dry, boring subject." Moreover, I have helped deliver this simulation in farm and ranch management classes with similar feedback from students.

Commodity Marketing

Dramatic changes are occurring that impact the agricultural, food, and fiber industries. As mentioned previously, policies change and globalization continues. These changes will make the markets for agricultural products such as wheat, corn, and cattle (agricultural commodities) more volatile in the future. Sellers of agricultural commodities are typically price takers (they take what the market price is) rather than price makers (they quote what they will sell their product for). The agricultural commodities and futures course that I teach is designed to educate students on a broad array of alternatives and price risk-management tools that can be used when marketing agricultural commodities. The course objectives are: (a) to give students a better understanding of commodity markets and commodity marketing, (b) to give students the expertise necessary to identify and evaluate marketing alternatives that can be used to manage price risk (volatility) and improve profitability, and (c) to give students a better understanding of how prices are determined in markets and the role futures markets play in that process.

The major concepts in this course relate to managing price risk or variability through using futures and options contracts, analyzing commodity markets, and cooperative or group marketing techniques. The market analysis portion of the course discusses the use of economic concepts such as supply (how much a producer is willing and able to produce at a given price), demand (how much a consumer is willing and able to purchase at a given price), and factor demand (how much a customer is willing to purchase an ag commodity for that will be used to produce a consumer-ready good). By understanding the theory behind these concepts, students can use information or indicators from the market that affect supply, demand, and factor demand as a way to predict potential price movement in commodity markets. Other indicators used from futures markets are also studied to help predict price movement and make decisions about when to buy and sell in the cash, futures, or options markets. The concepts are all discussed during the semester, and students are given a learning exercise in which they sell commodities in the current market situation. This exercise is designed to force the students to apply all that they have learned in both the marketing activity and writing up their results at the end of the semester.

For this activity, over an eight- or nine-week period students must use the course concepts to market commodities for "Mr. A.G. Ahporater." The student is placed in the following situation:

> You have decided to augment your exorbitant salary as a college student by moonlighting as a marketing specialist for Mr. A.G. Ahporater. Mr. Ahporater is diversified. He owns several farms and has a cow-yearling operation in southeastern Wyoming. A.G. has entrusted you with marketing 35,000 bushels of hard red winter wheat, 25,000 bushels of corn, and 140 head of steers from his herd that he has retained in a feedlot in western Nebraska.

> Mr. Ahporater had such good income from his cow-yearling operation this last year that he has waited to market the wheat and the corn until after the first of the year for tax purposes. A.G.'s corn did relatively well this year. His yields averaged 135 bushels to the acre, and his records show his costs of production plus land interest and real estate taxes were $297.60 per acre. Mr. Ahporater's dryland wheat ground averaged 29 bushels to the acre, and his variable costs of production plus interest and real estate taxes were $107.58 per acre. Anything made over these costs after marketing can be considered returns to management and labor.

> He placed the 140 head of steers in the feedlot October 20 this fall after marketing his culls and the yearlings he didn't retain. These cattle are in the "We Feed-Em Good" feedlot. The owners of the feedlot normally feed to choice (quality grade) slaughter weight.

They are good managers and have a record of 84 percent of their fed animals grading choice. These cattle are medium-frame black baldies, and the feedlot manager estimates that at 1,170 pounds live weight, before marketing, they all will drop from yield grade 3 to yield grade 4. He gives you some information on how the market has discounted yield grade 4 cattle relative to yield grade 3s. Given A.G. passed up $81.30/cwt for his steers, and an estimated feeding cost of gain of $51.16/cwt, the break-even price for these steers is estimated at $68.64/cwt. Additional cattle performance information is attached to the end of this report.

Your challenge is to market these commodities and try to return as much as possible to management and labor or reduce losses to management and labor.

Students are given additional cost and cattle performance data to use in their marketing decisions and the final report written to Mr. Ahporater. Moreover, students are given an online trading account which, when available for free to students, utilizes a simulation that uses ten-minute-delay real-time prices from the futures and options markets that actually trade contracts for these commodities. These markets are the CME Group (formerly known as the Chicago Mercantile Exchange and the Chicago Board of Trade) and the Kansas City Board of Trade (for more about this simulation, see www.commoditychallenge.com). The students then utilize the market information they find, making decisions about when and how much of a particular commodity to sell using futures contracts (called hedging), which futures contract to utilize, and when to market the commodity in the cash market. They keep track of all the marketing costs, including broker fees and transportation costs. At the end of the exercise, the students then compare the prices received from hedging in the futures market versus straight cash-marketing alternatives, and profits or losses for their strategies. They evaluate what they thought they did right in their marketing and what could be improved. Grades are based on the report, accuracy of the analysis of their strategies, and evaluation of what they thought they did well and what could be improved. As an additional incentive to improve the realism of the activity, I offer cash prizes to the top two marketers ($25 to first place and $15 to second place) in terms of overall profit for Mr. A.G. Ahporater. Research done by Chris Bastian, Larry VanTassell, Karen Williams, Dale Menkhaus, and Larry Held (1997) suggests providing monetary incentives can improve student interest. We did some experiments in class where students could win actual money in a commodity marketing class the better they did. The results indicated that the chance to win money created additional interest among students during the active-learning exercise.

During this activity, a number of teachable moments arise throughout the semester. Often these discussions involve students asking about why a market moved the way it did, or reinforcement of concepts already learned in class as relates to the mechanics of performing the actual marketing action and the costs and time involved. Students also seem to enjoy the competition for cash prizes. They often ask questions about who is in first place at any given time. Individual students' rankings regarding their current futures positions are sometimes posted on the online trading simulation, depending on which simulation software is used during the semester.

Even though this is a very involved exercise, most students seem to enjoy it and appreciate its applied nature regarding course concepts. Recent course evaluations included some of the following comments regarding what the strongest attributes of the course were: "Abundance of useful knowledge." "Real-life applications." "The marketing project was very worthwhile, and I learned a great deal of information from it." "…Really enjoyed the marketing project." "Very practical information." "Very informative—useful information, even outside aspect of ag commodities." "Applicability." These comments suggest the students got the "meat and potatoes" they were searching for. While these comments do not prove long-term educational impact, I have had a number of past students come to me and say they use what they learned in my class on their operation or at a current job. A recent e-mail communication from a student who took the class several years ago stated the following:

> I don't know if you remember me, but I took your futures and options class back in the spring of 2003. While I might not have remembered everything I learned in your class, I must have retained enough. I never thought in a million years when I was sitting in your class that I would use that information so much. I must have

learned enough to impress someone though, because I have just accepted a job from a company called _____ in Chicago. This company is one of the prominent futures and options brokers to the dairy industry. I just wanted to thank you for all your help and let you know that I wouldn't be in this position without that class.

Conclusion

The basic question asked at the beginning of this chapter was: How do college educators overcome the dilemma of teaching theory versus application? I believe the educational research done by experts and my experience both as a classroom instructor and former extension specialist point to the need students have to see how a concept or theory can be applied to a real-world problem. My approach to dealing with this issue is to teach the theory but provide ample examples and realistic experiential activities that draw on course concepts. The examples I have provided along with student feedback suggest this approach has merit. However, every instructor has to search for what works for him or her. I think the key for most new professors to remember is that their classroom is likely full of students who learn differently than they do. I don't believe professors have to forgo theory or rigor, but they cannot teach the theory or the concept to the exclusion of the application. There must be some balance struck that gives the greatest number of students the opportunity to understand the material and its application. That balance will likely be different for each instructor and across disciplines. I recognize that not everyone teaches the way I do, but for me, this is the way that seems to agree with my students and what I want to accomplish.

References

Bale, J.M., and D. Dudney. 2000. Teaching Generation X: Do andragogical learning principles apply to undergraduate finance education? *Financial Practice and Education* (Spring/Summer): 216–27.

Bastian, C., L. VanTassell, K. Williams, D. Menkhaus, and L. Held. 1997. Active learning with monetary incentives. *Review of Agricultural Economics* 19 (1): 475–83.

Briggs, K.C., and I.B. Myers. 1988. *Myers-Briggs type indicator: Form G.* Palo Alto, CA: Consulting Psychologists Press.

Brooks-Harris, J.E., and S.R. Stock-Ward. 1999. *Workshops: Designing and facilitating experiential learning.* Thousand Oaks, CA: SAGE Publications, Inc.

Capon, N., and D. Kuhn. 2004. What's so good about problem-based learning? *Cognition and Instruction* 22 (1): 61–79.

Caudron, S. 1997. Can Generation Xers be trained? *Training and Development* 51 (3): 20–25.

Coupland, D. 1991. *Generation X: Tales for an accelerated culture.* New York: St. Martin's Press.

Dunn, R., and K. Dunn. 1993. *Teaching secondary students through their individual learning styles: Practical approaches for grades 7–12.* Boston: Allyn and Bacon.

Horner, J.T., and L.A. Barrett. 1987. "Personality types of farm couples: Implications for intervention strategies." In H.G. Lingren et al., *Family Strengths 8-9: Pathways to Well-Being.* Lincoln, NE: Center for Family Strengths, University of Nebraska.

Jung, C.G. 1971. *Psychological types* (H.G. Baynes, trans. rev. by R.F.C. Hull). Vol. 6 of *The collected works of C.G. Jung.* Princeton, NJ: Princeton University Press. (Original work published 1921.)

Kolb, D.A. 1984. *Experiential Learning: Experience as the source of learning and development.* Englewood Cliffs, NJ: Prentice Hall.

McCarthy, J.P., and L. Anderson. 2000. Active learning techniques versus traditional teaching styles: Two experiments from history and political science. *Innovative Higher Education* 24 (4): 279–94.

Ricketts, J.C., F.R. Rohs, and G. Nichols. 2005. Learning modalities of agriculture students at a two-year agricultural college. *NACTA Journal* (December): 46–50.

Scott, P., and J. Zebrowski. 1998. Baby boomers teaching Generation X. www.isr.bucknell.edu/monterey/boomer/sld001.htm.

Schroeder, C. 1993. New students—New learning styles. *Change* (September–October): 21–26.

Weigel, R.R. 1999. The influence of personality on risk management decisions. *Risk and Resilience in Agriculture* (December) Article 6.4: 1–5. Published jointly by Colorado State University, University of Wyoming, and Montana State University Cooperative Extension Services.

3

David W. Wilson

D avid W. Wilson is a senior lecturer in the Department of Plant Sciences. He received his B.S. in agricultural production, with a horticulture option, from Montana State University in 1978. While directing the College of Agriculture Research Greenhouse Center, he completed an M.S. in agronomy from the University of Wyoming. His staff position was converted to an academic professional research scientist in 1993. He began teaching agroecology laboratories, winning an NACTA Graduate Student Teaching Award in his first year. In 1999, more teaching was added to his job description, and he was reclassified as an assistant lecturer. A year later he completed a Ph.D. from the University of Wyoming and was promoted to associate lecturer in 2001. He currently teaches six courses per semester in agroecology, horticulture, and graduate studies, as well as a summer-school field-studies course. He administers the agroecology apprenticeship and internship programs, and serves on college scholarship, honorary, and curriculum committees. He has sponsored agroecology laboratory teaching-methods workshops and contributed to various teaching-methodology events on campus.

Wilson has won writing awards for creative works such as "Outlaws in the Classroom," "Computerized Computer Eyes," and "Tracking Seeds from Space." "Dr. Dave" Wilson advises over half of the students in the agroecology degree program and received the "2006 Outstanding Advisor Award" in the College of Agriculture. He recently received numerous awards for teaching, including three UW Mortar Board "Top Prof" awards and an AGR "Props for Profs" award. He has been nominated for several outstanding-teaching awards within the college, university, and nation. With more than eleven different courses, he has consistently scored among the highest in student evaluations and faculty merit awards in his department. He has conducted research in weed science, seed science, horticulture, crop science, and organic production. Current grant work and graduate projects include studies in biofuels, biological control of nematodes and weeds, aquaponics, hydroponics, water conservation, high-tunnel greenhouses, wheat rotations, medic intercropping systems, and weed seed predation.

Trigger Tactics for Teaching

You would think with a father who taught high school shop and a mother who taught in a rural elementary school, I would have been prepared for my first semester of teaching. But in the fourth week of classes, I was already lost trying to decipher twenty-five handwritten lab reports. It wasn't just the illegible handwriting or even the frequent spelling errors. I was dumbfounded by the fact that a college student had done something I had thought impossible. While several students' reports contained minor grammatical errors, one student had actually managed to write a ten-word sentence without using a noun or a verb. He did, however, capitalize the first letter and punctuate his work—so I would know it was a sentence.

I was teaching a science lab, and at first I considered passing the buck. Why not let their college English professor correct the problem? Then, from pure ignorance and inexperience, I blamed the students, their prior education, and even their parents. Finally, I blamed myself and opted to try to do something. I corrected and graded the labs without penalizing for the writing errors. I handed the labs back in the next lab session, then announced that from now on, all labs must be typed and that no more than two spelling or grammatical errors would be accepted for credit. I would grade every lab, but they would have to redo labs with errors to receive full credit. In the next set of twenty-five neatly typed lab reports, there were no spelling or grammatical errors. I was delighted! However, on my evaluations I did receive one of my favorite six-word comments, with three spelling errors, "The lab reports wer to dificult."

Learning 'Triggers'

This story serves to inform the reader of my own level of unpreparedness, or maybe even naivete, concerning teaching. It did teach me that students will rise to benchmarks if they are clear and attainable. It also got me thinking of ways to "trigger" learning. When I refer to triggers, I'm really just using a term that encompasses various tricks and methods I've found useful to accomplish a desired effect. In the preceding example, the trigger was to establish a higher standard and a consequence if that standard was not maintained. It was not ignorance but laziness that correction. I've spent every semester since working on my trigger tactics. Some worked, some didn't. The successes stayed in the toolbox; the failures were modified or even discarded.

Most of my triggers developed by trial and error, until I stumbled on one that worked. Sometimes the trigger is simply a single word to get their attention. Not surprisingly, the word *sex* always seems to pull the most glassy-eyed student out of a stupor—even if it is only in reference to the transfer of pollen by a leafcutter bee to an alfalfa flower. Yet this was not something I inherently knew. My discovery of single-word triggers actually came about quite accidentally through an education college survey of student learning. During the semester-long survey period, ten students were pulled at random every two weeks and asked a set of questions. Although I was horrified they didn't remember everything I had tried to teach them, I was told I should be pleased because they had retained three times the amount of material as the test group in Biology 1000. However, the most glaring holes in their knowledge were all related to sexual reproduction. In retrospect, it was because I had falsely assumed that a college freshman probably already knew everything there was to know about sex. From this misperception, I had not included a single lecture on the subject of sex. I immediately inserted a series of lectures for the next semester to correct my error in judgment.

I modified one lecture into a discussion and created a cliff-hanger trigger. The topic given to the students on Monday for the discussion on Friday is titled "Sex and Energy," and it begins with a riddle, followed by four questions. The day they receive the assignment, I also add the challenge that no one has ever answered all five parts correctly. It is always a full room on Friday; most are there just to find out the answer to the riddle. The riddle reads:

> *If birds do it, fish do it, and bees do it…*
> *Even computer nerds do it…*
> *Do trees do it?*

I receive a multitude of guesses, some quite crude and some well thought out and partially correct. But imagine their shock to discover the entire answer to the riddle is the title of the homework. Since the previous lectures have already covered respiration (energy), we proceed to discuss the different mechanisms in plants for reproduction (sex) and answer the remaining four questions of the homework: Does grass have flowers? What is self-fertilization? Are there separate male and female plants within the plant kingdom? Why do plants need light, and what is produced in the presence of light?

I still employ benchmark triggers from time to time. Because exam scores can no longer be posted, all exams are returned individually, but along with the student's score a rank in the class is listed in the corner of the exam. Some students share their rank with friends, and invariably a competition develops between them. I have students post their group term papers in their student account, and then I provide an index to the Web pages, rank them in a sort of contest, and provide comments on each paper. Errors, such as spelling, drop a paper in the competition. I also remind the students that anyone in the world can read their work and that they will all need to read several of the papers for the final exam. It is an exercise in peer review and peer pressure. I was frustrated that there were still several spelling errors one semester on an individual Web assignment. Students were penalized one point per error, but it didn't seem to sink in because they didn't go back and correct the errors I had marked. I decided to break down all of the spelling errors by college and print out the results on an overhead. College of Arts and Sciences students won with zero errors from three students, the College of Business was second to last with six errors from thirty-four students, and the College of Education took last with thirteen errors from two students (three of which were the word *education*). Mentioning this impromptu survey in class resulted in immediate correction of all the spelling errors.

When striving for the goal of education and learning, it should almost be considered cheating not to teach a laboratory component in a course. I personally feel students learn far more in the lab environment than they could ever learn in a classroom. All courses should have a lab component, whether a formal hands-on science lab, problem set, or discussion. The reason for this is, again, "triggers." In the case of labs, tactile and olfactory sensory triggers come into play. While the standard lecture will use sight and sound, labs enable the use of smells and the chance for every student to see and touch what they are studying.

In lab students get dirty. And the dirtier they get, the more I expect they learn. One of the students' favorite labs every semester is the soil texturing lab. Students readily revert to their childhood of making mud pies. Playing in the mud has such wonderful tactile triggers. The main rule: everybody gets dirty. The soil particles students "feel" range in size from 0.002 to 2 millimeters in size and are broken apart into three categories: gritty, greasy, and sticky.

The sensation of touch is a powerful learning tool, one that my blind students taught me when they were able to correctly identify ten seeds and twenty plants based on touch alone. In the case of normal sighted students, vision may only confuse the situation. I frequently relate comments that my blind students have told me, telling their sighted classmates, "You can identify this plant with your eyes closed. It is the softest plant in the room." Or "Stroke the leaf toward the tip, it is smooth; pull down and it is rough."

Yes, labs are "hands-on." So it makes sense touch would come into play. But what about smell? There are actually two labs where smell plays the dominant role in explaining science. Both labs deal with microbes. In one lab, the microbes are the "good guys," soil microbes which allow nutrient and organic cycling. In the other lab, they are the "bad guys," which can cause plant disease. In the soil microbial lab, quart jars with soil, water, and one of four additives are prepared. The additives include sugar, sawdust, plant leaves, and cat food. After a week the jars are opened. While I take an electrical conductivity reading to determine the amount of CO_2 generated by the microbes, the students sniff the jars and record their best description of the smells.

A control (soil with only water added) should smell like soil after a rain. The jar with sugar added has a vinegary or bad wine smell, the plant leaves smell like a greenhouse, the sawdust smells like a musty cellar, and cat food generates a truly unique aroma. It is the cat food that waters eyes and weakens knees, much to my amusement. It is also the cat food that has earned such imaginative and descriptive labels as "really rank baby diapers in a pig pen." All of these memorable smells lead to an explanation of respiration, decomposition, fermentation, nutrient conversion, methane production, organic conversion, and the importance of an undisturbed, healthy microbial population in soil.

For the disease lab, a gamut of sensory triggers is used. Infection rates of *Rhizopus* fungus on six types of fruit are first evaluated visually and ranked from one to five. Students are then allowed to handle the fruit and rate them again. Finally, the ziplock bags are opened for an analysis by smell. The different fruits are then classified as either resistant or susceptible, followed by an open discussion of "why." In this sort of discussion, I sometimes have to inform the students that "they" must figure out the why. In early labs they sit silently, waiting for me to answer my own question. A trigger I use in this case is to tell them that every lab I've ever had has figured out the answers. This puts the pressure on them to perform as well as their peers. I should also mention that it is important in these types of discussions to find merit in every answer offered. A positive reception encourages students to respond in future labs. An additional lesson emphasized is the importance of using multiple and varied observations in any scientific analysis.

Even lab quizzes are sensory dependent. No "multiple-guess" bubble sheets in lab, nor lectures. Various types of lab quizzes are given throughout the semester. I like to mix it up, to test a more varied span of learning. One quiz requires studying the material and taking the quiz as soon as the student feels ready, a test of short-term memory. The other four quizzes occur the week following the lab during which the material is introduced, for a long-term memory test. Two of these quizzes are done by each individual and two as a group. The group quizzes are efforts in cooperation and, as open-book quizzes, are examples of observational, deductive reasoning. These are detective-type labs, and a trigger word to pique interest is to call them the "CSI" labs. Students will need to use their senses of sight, touch, and smell to complete any of these lab quizzes.

Accommodating Different Learning Types

There is a parallel between lab and lecture learning. That said, the more senses involved, the better the chance of information retention and learning. Many studies show differences in the way people learn. Is an individual right-brained or left-brained? Do they get their cues visually, through auditory stimulation, or from physical cues? It's not even that simple, since most people require two or more of these stimuli to learn. Stop and evaluate how you learn. Are these the only stimuli you use to teach others? I am an auditory learner. As a teacher, I might have done nothing but lecture, without a single visual aid. Luckily, I realized that although I remember what I hear, I don't retain what I see or read as well. But other people do use these learning stimuli. Therefore, I decided my lecture methods must utilize as many senses as possible.

For sight, overhead notes or slide text needs to be clear and concise. And for heaven's sake, black-and-white TVs have been gone for half a century. Color is required, especially for students who have been saturated in color since birth. Although it is a cliche, a picture really *is* worth a thousand words. Include pictures, lots of pictures that help reinforce the lecture notes. Visual stimuli are the easiest, and they affect the largest percentage of student learning triggers. For sound, speak up. Just like a professional singer, learn to project your voice clearly. I certainly can't put the blame on the students for sitting in the back row, especially when every seat in the room is filled. The average faculty lecturer is an introvert and therefore naturally quiet. Students will more than likely give up and stop coming to class, rather than say anything. Physical learners need activity. The instructor needs to move about, showing interest through animation and voice inflection. Students need the direct involvement of writing things down and asking questions. In a good lecture, all the senses are involved.

I have only recently started converting overhead lectures to slide shows. My reservations in doing so related to the unavailability or poor technology of the projector systems, more specifically, the low-light output of early computer projectors. Anything less than a thousand-foot-candle system requires turning the classroom lights off. When I attended classes in college, I watched class after class fall asleep during slide-show lectures. Guest lecturers in my own course have put half the class to sleep with a slide presentation. It was almost as if turning the lights down meant nap time. I refused to even try a slide-show lecture until the technology allowed the lights to remain on. Beyond the concept of poor lighting reducing student attention, the instructor loses the ability to read student expressions. Facial expressions are sometimes the only means (other than an exam) to measure comprehension versus confusion.

Importance of Observational Skills

I consider building observational skills so important that one-third of the lab grade is tied to a semester-long growth experiment. This simple class project requires daily and weekly examination, inspection, and monitoring of the study. Most critical is the ability to recognize what is normal growth and what is not. It may be as simple as an increase or decrease in growth, or it may be exhibited as mutations in leaf or stem shape, color changes, or flowering. Although a statistical analysis is required for every project, inclusion of observational notes about less quantifiable results shows a real understanding of science. For some students, this is the first time they have ever seen a plant grow. Yet it is sometimes these students, due to their intent interest, who make the best observers.

Normal versus abnormal growth is inherent in this laboratory research project. This is a definite hands-on learning experience. It is filled with tactile and visual triggers. Student observations lead to curiosity and questions. "Why are the stems red on some plants and not others?" "Why does that plant have yellow or white leaves?" The students learn the answers to specific questions, and I learn which students are the most interested in the project. Even better, some students answer their own questions. "Are the stems red due to phosphorus deficiency?" "Does a pale leaf mean the chloroplasts are dead or missing?"

On the first day of class, after groups are organized with a science leader, editor, statistician, and researcher, the following challenge is issued. Each group will conduct a phytotoxicity/phytoremediation study that has not been done previously by prior students. I refer to NASA experiments and use the Chernobyl nuclear accident as triggers to explain concepts. Explaining how sunflowers were used to remove radiation from the radioactive soil describes phytoremediation. I'm not sure why the acronym NASA is such an attention-getter, but they always seem to perk up when I talk about NASA's research with plants in space.

I continue with examples of previous studies and a background about not testing predictable results. Predictable results are explained as using products containing alcohol, salt, and oil, which will be bad for plants, and products containing hormones, nutrients, and water, which will be good for plants. Students face a challenging hour of group discussion to come up with something that may increase or decrease growth, has not been tested previously, and will not give a predictable result. I reject hundreds of materials as I visit with each group in rotation. To date, more than three hundred groups of students have come up with a unique test material.

Projects are set up the following lab period, but before that, I meet with science leaders to discuss hypotheses. My personal, and probably unpopular, belief is that hypotheses are not predictions. The word *prediction* is a simplified explanation of the word *hypothesis* and does not actually occur in the dictionary as a synonym or even as part of the definition for a hypothesis. The concept of a hypothesis being a prediction came about through the National Science Fair. It was an easy way to explain a complex concept to elementary-age students. It is the best example I know of a "bad trigger." The word *prediction* imparts an aspect of bias. Predicting means we are guessing that we know what might happen. Students who treat a hypothesis as a prediction usually state in their final report that the research proved them wrong or right. "I was right," and science proves it. Is it any wonder that in a society that expects science to solve its problems, science is distrusted?

Back to the Basics: Biology

It was years before I discovered students were not required to take a biology course in many high schools. This meant most students had never been exposed to many of the science terms used to explain biology. The limited biology vocabulary they retained was from their elementary education. I worked at developing vocabulary triggers to decrease the steep learning curve. It was an aspect of teaching the language of science to enable learning of concepts. Although it was already apparent that some students had difficulty mastering English, this meant teaching Latin too. Teaching the Latin root of a biological term was the only way to lower the learning curve. This was going to require a trigger to help students overcome terms they had difficulty remembering.

The first biologic terms students encounter in lab are seed terms such as *monocotyledon, dicotyledon,* and *polycotyledon.* Students already know that *mono* means one, as in monorail, *di* means two, and *poly* means many. I don't need triggers for the first set of terms. The three related terms are simply explained and learned as one, two, and many cotyledons. But germination is divided into either *epigeal* or *hypogeal*, and I need triggers like *epidermis* and *hypodermic*. These are terms students have heard but maybe don't understand. Once it is explained that the epidermis refers to their skin, which is on the outside of their body, and that a hypodermic needle is used to place something under the skin, the two germination terms can be more easily remembered. Epigeal germination is when the cotyledons are pulled outside of the soil, while hypogeal germination is when the cotyledons remain under the soil surface. This lab continues with terms such as *hypocotyl* and *epicotyl*, now simple to learn, since they share common Latin roots with the previous terms. The terminology list builds with *coleoptile, coleorhiza, radicle,* and *endosperm.*

After this initial exposure to some Latin roots, the same triggers are used in lecture. A new term requires a definition, the Latin root, and trigger words to which a student can relate and build understanding. For example, two terms to explain how organisms derive energy are *autotrophic* and *heterotrophic.* Latin roots translate *trophic* to a feeding relationship, *auto* to self, and *hetero* to other. The important concept for a student to remember is which is which. There is not a common term to relate to *trophic,* but both terms relate to how organisms attain nourishment. Therefore, a trigger for the commonality of the terms is not as critical. The trigger words *automobile* and *heterosexual* are used to allow students to sort the differences. An automobile is a means of self-conveyance, therefore an autotroph is an organism which is self-feeding, such as a plant, which uses inorganic sunlight to make energy. A heterosexual is attracted to the other sex, as a heterotroph is attracted to others for nourishment, in other words, organisms eating other organisms of either living or dead organic matter.

Using the same methods in labs and lectures to build vocabulary enhances learning in both. I am not speaking of redundancy; I prefer to call these ties between labs and the lecture "loop learning"—that ability to say, "Remember last lab when...," "Do you recall the lecture we spoke about ...," or "Tell me how this relates to discussion." I understand a student's problem of understanding biology when they can't speak the language. I have a similar problem in understanding rap music. The learning curve is steep, and without an understanding of the terminology, they don't have the tools to get to the top. From personal experience, I remember how stupid I felt when my father-in-law explained how a computer was built. Within minutes my eyes glazed over in confusion. But I was interested, and so I learned the terminology and went on to bore other people with my explanations of the wonders of hardware and electrical engineering.

Singing in Class and Other 'Taboos'

I have mentioned using the word *sex* as a trigger twice previously. There are many other cultural preoccupations available, and many come from the pop culture of movies and songs. Pop culture stars can evoke strong learning responses; the trick is to find one who evokes the same response for everyone. For example, a political commentator may give a strong response, but it can be in two completely opposite directions and difficult to channel. Second, the pop star must be prevalent in the same generation as the students. Paulie Shore was funny in his stereotypic movie roles of a bumbling, burned-out hophead. Today he is just that failed, older comedian from the 1990s. Singer-actress Jessica Simpson presents the opportunity to stress the importance of education until someone points out she made millions without a high school diploma. My rule is to stay away from politicians and only use a pop star or an athlete who has recently made headlines. Otherwise, stick with positive historical triggers such as the genius of Einstein, honesty of Lincoln, ingenuity of Carver, and bravery of Crockett. No matter how funny it might be to talk about quail hunting with the vice president, it won't get you a universal response.

I have even broken out in song during class. Not often, but sometimes, the right phrase just seems better in a song. I've always been embarrassed afterward, but truthfully, I wish I were a better singer. It's such a great trigger. "Hey, Susan. What was he singing about today?" "Say, John. Do you remember that song he sang about photosynthesis? How does that go again?" Alas, I can't rap, and so I am relegated to William Shatner–type ballads. If only Willie Nelson could stop in for a visit, sing a song or two, and talk about Farm Aid.

The true trigger words that get a drifting student's attention fall into taboo areas. The top four: sex, drugs, alcohol, and tobacco. Just the mention of the Bureau of Alcohol, Tobacco and Firearms draws attention or gets a snicker. I've never understood how the word *tobacco* piques interest. Nicotine is an addictive carcinogen, and I generally only use the word to draw attention to the toxicity of nicotine. Nicotine is an insecticide, nicotine is near the top of the EPA LD$_{50}$ toxicity table, and nicotine was a driving force for the colonization and agriculturalization of the Americas. Oops, so even something with so many negative aspects may have its positives.

Such is the case with alcohol. Movies like *Animal House* and many similar films since then have perpetuated and popularized campus life as one big party. It is as big a problem on campuses as drunken driving is on our streets and highways. It is something our culture must acknowledge and deal with through various disciplinary and educational measures. But I won't pretend it doesn't exist, and I will use the word *beer* as a trigger. It is the best attention-grabber when lecturing about anaerobic respiration in plants and bacteria. If I want students to remember the equations and cycles of respiration, anaerobic respiration is the easiest when students are told to think of beer. Anaerobic respiration is also known as fermentation, and its by-products are alcohol and carbon dioxide.

Beyond the fact that beer was invented by the Babylonians as a means of curing nutritional and vitamin deficiencies, the beer industry employs a large portion of students after graduation. From my perspective, it is the perfect poster child to explain chemical relationships in plants. It is valuable for explaining fermentation and the concepts of phytoremediation and phytotoxicity. Yet there is a hidden message. Phytoremediation and phytotoxicity studies determine the tolerance levels of plants to a substance. Beer was studied the first semester I taught lab as a graduate student. Beer is 95 percent water and 5 percent alcohol. Small quantities of beer actually benefited plants (much like the Babylonians), but large quantities were toxic. The message is: too much of anything is usually bad for you.

Active Discussions

As educators, our job is to inform students and let them make their own decisions. Therefore, our own philosophies about such things as politics and religion have no place in most classrooms. Yet a discussion session needs dissent. There is no discussion if everyone is in agreement. And the goal is not to make everyone think the same. Several years ago my discussion sessions were featured as part of a teaching symposium. One instructor approached me afterward and said, "I understand the concept of discussions, but I don't understand how you do it." I was quite confused by the statement. It seemed if you understood the concept, the "how" was automatic. I tried to answer her question by describing how to control the flow of the discussion. She seemed perplexed but remained quiet, and we parted ways. I later found out, from students, that she used discussions to mold students toward a single set of beliefs. Her discussions began argumentatively and ended in silence. Triggers can be used to direct the flow without restraining thought.

I have discovered several triggers for discussions. Standing quietly behind or near a group presenting a counterpoint draws attention and validity to the students' presentation. Students tend to follow the instructor, and my standing near the orator draws their attention to the student. A discussion is worthless unless every student's opinion is considered and thought to have merit. For the most part, I try to act as a moderator calling for points and rebuttal but occasionally interjecting a trigger, something to stimulate or direct the discussion. My expectations include the ability of a student to defend an opinion and the ability of any student to change his or her opinion. I remember a student having a difficult time defending her position. She kept saying, "That's just the way it should be *because!*"—without ever giving any reasons to support her position. When pushed, she admitted that she didn't know any reasons to do it that way. She just felt it was what society wanted her to believe. She failed to defend her position but stood up and moved to another group, showing an even rarer ability to change her opinion.

A student's name is a trigger. Knowing every student's name is part of the one-on-one exchange needed to stimulate learning. The way their faces brighten up when you call on them is worth the effort and time it takes to learn each name. I take digital photos in lab to create a thumbnail file spreadsheet of photos and names. I study the spreadsheet and keep it nearby during lab. Usually, by the fifth week I have learned all seventy names. I probably couldn't do it as quickly without teaching lab sections, although hand-delivering assignments in lecture helps. Individually delivering assignments allows me to walk around the classroom, learn names, and spend some time with each individual student.

One of the best triggers I've ever used in discussion requires a second collaborator. I normally write topics to create four discussion groups. On one occasion, the topic yielded two groups. I then talked another instructor into coming to class, and we worked out a good cop, bad cop routine. I sat with one group and she sat with the other, helping them defend their opinion. The trigger came halfway through the class, as we both got up and switched positions. We now became as dedicated to the point we currently defended as we were opposed to it a minute before. The expression on the students' faces was priceless. The one drawback of this technique was that it required the two of us to be more vocal than I would like. The positive was that the students realized there really were two sides to every issue.

The students love discussions. I love discussions. They don't always go as planned, but I know I have succeeded when the last question asked is, "So, what do you think?" That they don't know where I stand means I did it right. Sometimes they assume what my position is on an issue. This is not to say that I express my opinion, only that I have probably helped one group more than another and the result is that they assume I agree with that group. I've found no matter how hard I try, students will make certain assumptions. It may come from a misunderstanding of something I've said, their own desire that I believe what they believe, or even that I remind them of someone in their past experience (good or bad). Such preconceptions have always been the greatest barrier to learning in my classroom experience.

The Ultimate Trigger

Finally, I will give away my greatest secret weapon, a trigger so powerful it shouldn't be legal. Again, my discovery was entirely by accident and one that would only work for a handful of people. I teach a science course that conflicts with the beliefs of conventional agricultural society. This means that everything I say is immediately questioned if it is not the way it is done back home on the farm. I didn't realize it at the time, but I needed a way to break some deeply rooted preconceptions. One of my hobbies at the time was historical reenactments. I had never had a problem with hair length, and although mine was always short I decided to grow it out for an event that summer. I left it long through the summer, and once school started, I considered cutting it off but didn't. Within a few weeks that semester, I discovered something unusual. There was less resistance to the sustainable farming methods

I proposed. The same methods that had been scoffed at previously were now being embraced as an obviously better way of doing things.

Okay, so maybe the first visual here is one of Samson and the Philistines, or maybe an impression that the long hair just allowed the students to identify with the instructor. The answer was actually nothing quite so obvious and did not become clear to me until I read the student evaluations and had conversations with students once the semester was over. The evaluations were clear: the hair had gained critical notice. Some simply wrote, "He needs a haircut," or "Nice hair." Buried in the frivolous comments that had nothing to do with education were the comments that exposed the truth. Perceptions had been broken. Their first impression was that I was some sort of long-haired environmentalist radical, or a rock star. Within weeks they discovered I was knowledgeable about and supportive of agriculture. They learned I was from a farm and had been involved in agriculture since I was 8. This realization that things were not always what they seemed made them stop, think, and listen.

My favorite comment was from a senior I overheard telling my department head that on his first day of my class, he took one look at my hair and decided it was going to be a worthless semester. I immediately leaned closer to overhear the conversation. This Georgia farm boy continued, "I hadn't ever seen anyone with hair that long. But two weeks later I realized I better start paying attention, because this guy really knew something." Relieved, I sat down with the pair, and the student proceeded to tell how on his last visit home his uncle had asked him, "What in the hell is this agroecology stuff, anyway?" He knew his uncle's operation and proceeded to explain to my department head, in detail, all the ways his uncle could improve his farm. All that my department head could say to him was, "Wow, you really learned your stuff!" Then he smiled and nodded at me. To me that moment was like the commercial, "Priceless." There was a brief silence and the student added, "My dad is coming to graduation, and he's really going to hate your hair when he sees you." The student became a crop consultant in Georgia and still calls me today. Will I cut my hair anytime soon? My Delilah will come the day I retire.

4

Stephen Earl Williams

Stephen Earl Williams is professor of soil science in the Department of Renewable Resources at the University of Wyoming (UW) and director of Wyoming's Reclamation and Restoration Center. He entered academe as a faculty member in 1976 when he joined the Department of Plant Sciences. In 1988 he became a member of the Department of Plant, Soil and Insect Sciences, and in 1993 was selected to head that department. In 1998, he was appointed dean of the UW Graduate School, where he served for five years. During this one-institution career, he has maintained a research program largely in soil biology and specifically soil microbiology, specializing in microorganisms that occupy plant roots and enhance plant growth. This work has application to disturbed land restoration at numerous levels, including mine land reclamation and more recently in evaluation of climate change impacts in alpine ecosystems. While at UW, Williams has taught Soil Taxonomy, Forest and Range Soils, Introductory Soil Science, Soil Microbiology, Soil Biology and Biochemistry, Environment and Society, the Capstone Course in Agroecology, various seminars, and special topics courses including, recently, a graduate-level course in Microbial Ecology. His formal academic training was at New Mexico State University (Las Cruces) for a bachelor's in biology (minor in chemistry) and a master's in agronomy (minor chemistry), and at North Carolina State University (Raleigh) for a Ph.D. in soil science (minor in microbiology).

Organized Doubt

Instructors are faced with presenting mega-gigabytes of information to students who are expected to, and sometimes want to, assimilate and understand that information. There is so much information to lecture on that little time remains to discuss its origin, controversy, or accuracy. Often the objective is to cover the information linearly and quickly, and move on. Information and even concepts thus come off as absolutes—above argument or question. But the constants used in chemistry and physics are estimates, not absolutes. Distances used in geography are similarly estimates, not absolutes. As a result, the concepts derived from information are necessarily incomplete or approximate. Relativity is a theory, not a law; evolution is a theory, not an absolute.

To teach concepts as absolutes is fraught with pitfalls as students realize such concepts may be based on estimates or seemingly contradictory information. Anyone should challenge such concepts when they seem contrary to logic or closely developed beliefs. Such challenges can lead to conflict and discussion that is at best circular and at worst destructive and misleading. But it can also lead to conflict and discussion that can be of considerable interest, spawning enlightenment. However, an instructor often finds himself or herself on the defensive as he or she tries to prove to a student or set of students that his or her argument trumps conflicting arguments or beliefs. Such discussions become more focused and logical if *organized doubt* is established as the mechanism whereby arguments can be considered and dissected. Organized doubt is the basis for scientific investigation specifically and all academic inquiry in general. The process of establishing central questions, deriving hypotheses from those questions, and testing those hypotheses is at the core of any argument where alternative outcomes are in the offing. Fundamental in discussion (in spite of the oxymoron) is that absolute proof is absolutely not possible! The approach of attempting to disprove a null hypothesis, and this is the heart of organized doubt, provides a means for examining even complex and controversial issues. This approach provides a mechanism to organize and discuss questions. More importantly, this approach is a sorting device, categorizing questions into those that yield to doubt and those that do not.

However, the use of the null hypothesis comes with provisos: mainly that one has to admit imperfect knowledge and further recognize that the society of *Homo sapiens* does not know everything.

In the end, care must be taken when using the null hypothesis and organized doubt, especially with less experienced students. 'Tis amazing how subtlety and indirectness can catch the attention of students.

The Null Hypothesis and the Lack of Absolutes

In the room the women come and go
Talking of Michelangelo.

(From T.S. Eliot's "The Love Song of J. Alfred Prufrock," 1919)

"DNA is the carrier of genetic information." "*Rhizobium leguminosarum* is the prokaryotic agent of nitrogen fixing cortical hypertrophies on peas." "Selenium absence in the diet is the cause of a nutritional muscular dystrophy." These are all examples of concepts and information often taught as absolutes. Why do we teach them as absolutes? We have slithered into a trap—we the teachers, too, think they are absolutes, and we think we have proved, for example, that DNA is the carrier of genetic information. But we must always be excruciatingly aware that science is not based on proof! Sure, we can mathematically prove that the sum of the angles of a triangle equals 180 degrees. However, in most of our work we do not prove! Instead, *our confidence in a particular concept is based on our inability to disprove.* I know to students this sounds like some kind of ivory tower, mumbo jumbo baloney. But whether learners are freshmen or Ph.D. candidates, technicians or faculty, janitors or presidents, they benefit and society benefits from their applying the tenets of *organized doubt.* I argue here that most of the misconceptions related to science are a result of failure to organize doubt and appropriately doubt. Consider the example of DNA again.

In 1953, James D. Watson and Francis H.C. Crick proposed a chemical structure for deoxyribonucleic acid (DNA). They based their model on published information developed by others, and published their model. The model represented their *hypothesis.* By publishing their hypothesis, Crick and Watson were asking the global community of investigators to test the model for validity. A lot of information supported their model, including Erwin Chargaff's rules (see account in Campbell and Reece 2005) and Rosalind Franklin's x-ray defractions (see account in Watson 1968; also see Crick 1962). Others professionally challenged the model experimentally; notable among these was Kornberg (1962). He posed the question that the Watson and Crick model was not the structure of DNA, and organized his experimentation around this null hypothesis. *Hypothesis:* the Watson and Crick model is the correct model for DNA. *Null hypothesis:* the Watson and Crick model is not the correct model for DNA. Essentially he sought data to support the null hypothesis, and designed and carried out elaborate and exhaustive experiments to find fundamental flaws in the Watson and Crick model. His null hypothesis was a statement of his professional doubt of the fundamentals of the Watson and Crick model. As an investigator, his professional responsibility was to doubt the model, but, further, it was his professional obligation to provide information that supported his doubt. Thus did Kornberg contribute to our current knowledge of and confidence in the Watson and Crick model—he doubted and organized his doubt to address their hypothesis. More to the point, he was unable, by experimentation, to generate an argument that supported his null hypothesis—and his doubt. More succinctly, he disproved the null hypothesis. Even more important, by implication, he failed to disprove the Watson and Crick model (or hypothesis).

The temptation is to go a step further and say that Kornberg proved the Watson and Crick model. Kornberg provided information that at best supported the Watson and Crick model. It did not prove or provide proof of the Watson and Crick model! Dozens if not hundreds of other experimenters have *organized doubt* to address the validity of the Watson and Crick model. To date there is little evidence to support the null hypothesis. To date a vast body of evidence does not support the null hypothesis. As a consequence, in our closely guarded beliefs about the fundamental nature of the universe, we as investigators think the Watson and Crick model represents the actual, true structure of DNA! Still, every genetic experiment that is performed is, in some way, a continued organized effort to doubt the Watson and Crick model. Someone may yet find data to support the null hypothesis. And if he or she does find that data, and if others confirm, does this mean that the whole proposed structure of DNA comes tumbling down? Maybe, but likely it will provide the basis for a revised structure, a new hypothesis, a new null hypothesis, and a new set of experiments based on the premise of organized doubt. Thus does the community of doubters place another stitch in the fabric that represents our combined knowledge. Yes, the fabric is continuously partially unraveled and stitched again, and there is always the chance that carefully constructed organized doubt will rip the fabric asunder. If that happens, we should rejoice for from such rips comes enlightenment, from such doubt comes understanding of the essence of our existence and our relationship with the universe.

Have such rips in fabric of accepted knowledge occurred before? Yes—many, many times. Has such revolution come easily and been easily accepted? Absolutely not! The names of the revolutionaries are written across the sticky clay of history as lines of societal condemnation, pain, and excommunication. Their names ring down through the halls of history, fill basins with tears, elicit disdain, but ultimately provide illumination: Kepler, Galileo, Newton, Darwin, Curie, Meitner, and Carson, to name a few.

The objective of this brief treatment of the null hypothesis is to suggest that in the classroom we err on the side of absolutes, when there are in fact no absolutes. Although this paper will provide a little of the classical background on who developed the use of the null hypothesis and why it was developed, my objective is to present several avenues of consideration that cores of argument in the classroom, argument in the courtroom,* societal arguments, and international discussion should be strongly undergirded by doubt! The scientific method is an expression of organized doubt and techniques to analyze that doubt. We are a society that looks for absolutes, seeks proofs, and demands no risk. These expectations are inconsistent with observations, our knowledge of probability, and the decision-making methodology painstakingly established since the Renaissance. This methodology is summarized as the process of asking questions, formulating hypotheses, and then testing those hypotheses via evaluation of null hypotheses. To ignore this fundamental evaluative philosophy is to deny the

---

*It is interesting to note that in academics especially we routinely assign a probability to certainty or doubt (e.g., $P \leq 0.05$) whereas in the courtroom, juries and witnesses are often instructed more qualitatively to base judgment on evidence "beyond a reasonable doubt." A huge conflict of cultures potentially results, and does result, when issues of science are decided in the courtroom. A classic case here is the Scopes Trial of 1925 (Grebstein 1960).

fundamentals of how the universe functions. To attend to this philosophy provides us the means to address even the most perplexing classroom questions, provides us opportunity to address questions "to which there is no technical solution" (Hardin 1968), and provides an avenue for rational decision making. By no means is the method foolproof or can it be used to evaluate all questions. The salient point is that fairly quickly with the scientific method, one can distinguish between those questions that lend themselves to organized, intense scrutiny and those that do not.

History, Data, and Observation

The ancient Greek philosopher Thales of Miletus is credited with deriving the idea of "first principles." He, or probably more accurately, the thinkers of his time are responsible for two major realizations. The initial one is that there is some principle, probably some physical substance, that explains or is the fundamental building block of everything else. Thales proposed the first principle was water.

This was a good observation. He noted that water was in a lot of things and had a lot of different faces (phases). He could turn water into steam and could see that when it condensed, it was water again. He noted that water could be turned into a solid but with a little heat could become liquid water again. He undoubtedly noted that one could squeeze fruit, and the liquids expressed had a watery component. Blood had a lot of water in it. It seems likely that to Thales, stones, wood, bone, and much more were just physical manifestations of water that he had not figured out yet (Van Doren 1991).

The second, and probably more pervasive and important, realization by Thales and his generation was that the mind of man could figure out and understand nature. Sure, Thales was in part incorrect about water. Sure, water is made up of atoms, and other Greeks derived the notion that the physical world was made up of the "uncuttable or indivisible": that if meat, stone, wood, or any substance was cut finely enough, it finally reached a level where is was not further cuttable and was thus uncuttable. Thus the derivation of the term *atom*, meaning indivisible or uncuttable (Van Doren).

Of course the Greeks did not know that atoms were cuttable to electrons, neutrons, and protons. Only more recently did we find that these were further cuttable to other sub-subatomic particles. But still, it is monumental to think that the mind of man could grope with, figure out, and understand nature. Of course, as this notion began to bear a better understanding of nature, the detail of nature, and the intricate beauty and architecture thereof, this also spawned humility, especially among those who studied nature in depth. Unfortunately it also bolstered arrogance, but it is probable that arrogance was rampant long before Thales.

The Myth of the Cave

One of the most perceptive and frustrating narratives in science philosophy also comes from ancient Greece. This is connected strongly to observations of early philosophers such as Thales. His greatest contribution may have been that he perceived nature as something that could be understood because it followed logical and predictable patterns. However, the narrative illustrates metaphorically the ambiguous nature of nature, the distortion of the information that we acquire on the nature of nature, and the limited powers we have to observe and process information. But if we accept the idea that we have the capacity to understand the world and universes around us, and if we admit that we do not yet understand everything, it also means that we have observations yet to make and interpretations left to generate. Our world and the decisions we make about our world continue to hinge more and more on the accumulated knowledge of our species or the fabric of knowledge that stretches across disciplines and transcends time. Often we assume that our storehouse of knowledge stands on an unshakable foundation. Only with a deeper understanding of the roots of our knowledge and our science do we come to know that the fabric of knowledge has many holes and that even the existing fabric is fragile and in places flimsy.

Somewhere on the path from Athens to Sparta, the trail passes through a fairly long and dark cave. All of society and much more must pass through this cave. Because the cave is so dark, there are fires lit periodically along its length, but exclusively on one side of the path and not the other. For on the other side of the path, in a position slightly below the grade of the path, reside the observers: the scientists, the sociologists, the humanists, the philosophers. Here they are positioned such that they can only see the wall of the cave and they can see only the dark forms, the shadows, projected on the wall by the fires behind. And from the shadows on the wall, they must discern all of what is happening in nature. And from this information they are charged with making decisions that affect the physical, mental, and biological health of their society. They determine what foods should be grown, how much wine to make, who should be the gatekeepers, what new technologies should be pursued, if dams should be built, and if wars should be fought. Some projections on the cave wall are distinct—an oxcart loaded with women, men, and children. But others are indistinct—the subtle change in light intensity as it passes through a vapor. And from this limited data, we who learned from those who sat with the ancient Greek observers, and now ourselves seated and pondering the cave wall, must continue to conjecture about nature (Plato ca. 385 BC).

From antiquity we have actually been seemingly successful in this endeavor. From the faintest traces in cloud chambers and minute attractions between bodies has come atomic theory that seems to explain most of chemistry and some of physics. From a few x-ray diagrams, a little knowledge of biology, and a couple of stoichiometrically equivalent molecular weights has come the structure of deoxyribonucleic acid, which seems to explain part of biology. This is the powerful metaphor inherent in the Greek "myth of the cave" (Plato). It haunts all of science and is the source of many errors as we bumble through the laboratories and the natural world trying to reduce complex data and observation into something that we can take in through our feeble senses. But even in the face of our own limitations, we are still confronted with our own arrogance and the difficulty of multifaceted problems with no apparent technical solution (see Hardin).

"What ever do you mean by that, Thrasymachus?

(From Plato's *The Republic,* ca. 385 BC)

College Teaching: A Primer

The above is mostly a review of the very basic philosophy that serves as a foundation for scientific methodology. The scientific method does have limitations as a problem-solving tool and becomes cumbersome when used to resolve multifaceted, complex problems that are often nonlinear, massively dimensional, and associated with the functioning of human society. This chapter is an attempt to shed a little light on the process, culture, and techniques of teaching. The scientific method can be used in this effort but can be awkward and ponderous.

A fundamental piece of any inquiry is establishment of the hypothesis or the central question for investigation. Any effort toward inquiry or investigation proceeds more completely and successfully when it is based on a carefully considered question. Statistical methods have been developed for honing in on critical questions. In qualitative research, there are lines of inquiry where interview questions are allowed to emerge while the observer puts his or her own biases and notions aside. In more uses of the scientific method, employment of "multiple working hypotheses" (Chamberlin 1890) helps the investigator to hone in and focus ultimately on central questions, but allows consideration of a broader set of questions. These are exceptionally important topics for advanced students such as graduate students.

Many undergraduate students come to the university with a distorted view of hypothesis testing, and this is based almost entirely on a highly distorted view of hypothesis generation and science as a whole. This usually has been sorted out by the time a student enters graduate school, but a large majority of undergraduate students leave school with their degrees along with a retarded or overinflated understanding of science and its methodology.

I have had the opportunity for more than ten years to participate as a sweepstakes judge in the Wyoming State Science Fair. This means that annually I have the opportunity to view the several top senior science fair projects in each of a dozen categories. This is a huge challenge, but fortunately I have had a lot of help from experts in each of the categories as well as the other sweepstake judges who aid in this process.

A fundamental characteristic of almost all high school science fair projects that we see is that they seldom test hypotheses. Usually the projects are demonstrations, product tests, or displays. When science fair students attempt to use the scientific method in their work, efforts are routinely ill conceived and often focused on proving a point rather than failing to support the converse of that point.

A compelling argument is, therefore, that even the best of our high school students are ignorant as to the workings of scientific methodology. This suggests that their teachers likely are in the same clueless category. To take this one more step, this situation implies that the high school teachers were not well versed or versed at all in scientific inquiry in their own educational experience. Of course, the finger points then at us, the teachers at university who taught the high school teachers! We too often seem clueless where standard inquiry is concerned. My contention is that we tend to teach toward the glitz of science and do not teach toward the philosophical underpinnings of science. Our students leave the university thinking that computers, DNA kits, inductively coupled plasma units, mass spectrometers, and especially PowerPoint all represent the core of science. These are only tools and techniques. They are not science!

Even in modern, fundamental biology textbooks, the philosophical underpinnings of biological experimentation are largely ignored. Three recent and very popular biology textbooks (Campbell and Reece 2005; Freeman 2005; Raven et al. 2005) do address hypothesis testing. The first allocates two pages, and the second and third each allocate three pages. Freeman even spends half a page on the null hypothesis. Each of these books has about 1,250 pages (and each weighs about 3.2 kilograms) as well as an accompanying CD-ROM and Web site. More damning, however, is that there are essentially no references in these textbooks that point the reader, the student, to the original works that form the foundations of these texts! Yes, they credit photos and graphics from original research, but they do not cite original works.

By comparison, a biology text from 1963 (Weisz) provides eight and a half pages on the "procedure of science" that is entirely on the process of hypothesis synthesis, testing, and restatement. It does not speak to the null hypothesis, but it has other attributes. It is only 786 pages long, is well referenced, does not come with CD or Web site, and weighs a slender 1.7 kilograms. A further comparison is a biology text from 1929 (Wells et al.) that provides no formal explanation of hypothesis testing (1,480 pages, 1.5 kilograms, no CD or Web site, but also no references). It does address "the incontrovertible fact of evolution" in about one hundred pages of text including considerable proof that evolution is correct and creationism is not! Organization and evolution of textbooks have come a long way since 1929, but there seems to be recent, retrograde tendencies at work, especially in citation of fundamental work. It is also clear that some biology text writers probably would do better in the area of science fiction!

It is very important that, especially at the college level, information and examples of hypothesis testing and examples of null hypotheses are provided in textbooks. Further, it is important that a fairly clear demarcation is established between those conclusions we are pretty sure about ($P \leq 10^{-6}$) and those where we are not ($P \leq 0.49$). Where such hypotheses, null hypotheses, or demarcations are not provided, it is the obligation of the instructor to do so.

The intention here is not to be overly critical of the writers and publishers of textbooks. After all, there is a lot of information to convey, there are publics to attend to, and money to be made! I would nevertheless contend that the colored pictures and graphs, interviews and examples, bindings and slick pages all miss the point of organized doubt, of the essence and heartbeat of investigation, and the source of this kind of knowledge.

We as a modern society, whatever that means, are condemned by attitudes toward knowledge, the most fatal being arrogance! That we know it all or that we do not need to know—both ideas are fatal. What we think of as science is part of the problem too. Massive rocket ships pushing cargoes to Mars and beyond, submarines cruising the ocean bottoms and mapping details never thought imaginable, ultraclean laboratories where genetically modified organisms are grown, cycloramic or linear accelerators where subatomic particles are smashed—all of this seems like science, but I would contend it is not science. It may be the trappings of science, the garb of science, but it is not the core of science! The core, the strength, the fundamental principle upon which all of science is based is still *organized doubt.*

The Generation of Hypotheses

The stereotyped image of the researcher is of some eccentric bald-headed male deep in the laboratory among the paper sacks of samples, microscopes dripping with scientific specimens, the hum of an AutoAnalyzer, trays of mounted specimens, and piles of inane and arcane literature. Indeed, some of the stereotype is accurate. But many well-respected researchers have little more than an office and a computer. Their data comes over the Internet or might be collected in field settings. Their laboratories may be the symposium chamber, their motel room, or the state of their residency.

And the questions they research are not necessarily brain explosions that come to their minds suddenly. Instead, they are questions generated by dozens of colleagues working and communicating over periods of time that may span generations and cross geographical distances sometimes, but not always, limited only by the dimensions of the planet. These questions may start as vague notions or gut ruminations. Often before they are expressed in testable hypothesis terms, they may take on dimensions of a central hypothesis.

> *Peering out between the branches of the venerable plant,*
> *We all saw the surrounding landscape differently.*

> (From S.E. Williams's "Tangled," 1997)

In my own discipline, soil science, a central hypothesis is the soil state equation. Hans Jenny (1941) was the first to articulate this conceptual principle. Jenny is as important to ecosystem scientists as Albert Einstein is to physical scientists.

Jenny, like Einstein, was born in Europe and driven from that fertile and diverse land by the failure of technical solutions to solve societal problems. The United States has been the recipient of many such immigrants fleeing war, pestilence, politics, or famine and coming to reside and contribute here.

Professor Jenny too derived an equation, and like Einstein's famous equation, it was conceptual and theoretical. It too explains much and connects universes of knowledge thought previously to be unconnected.

To understand Jenny's equation requires some rather deep understanding of ecology and of the place of soil in ecology. Basically the equation suggests that soil is a transforming interface between the universe of geology and the universe of biology, between the universe of the living and the universe of the dead, and between the terrestrial gases, liquids, and solids. It is a place of intense chemical and physical activity where the physical and chemical action of temperature, the many physical states of water, and the many chemical manifestations of water act to tear down and build up inorganic solids and the organic matrix that constitutes soil.

As indicated previously, the soil state equation is a conceptual equation. At its most fundamental level, it suggests soil is a function of geological materials (often called, euphemistically, parent material), climate, organisms, and topography. The duration of the interaction of these four factors is also a factor and in Jenny's equation is simply called "time." The soil state equation is often simplified into something that resembles mathematics. However, we know so little quantitatively about soil that the mathematical expression of the soil state equation is more like the expression of equations in quantum mechanics. That is, we do not know enough about the topic to solve the equation for the factor variations and ensuing combinations.

The soil state equation: $S = F\,(\text{PM, Cl, Org, Topo})_T$

And it reads: Soil (S) is a function (F) of parent material (PM), climate (Cl), organisms (Org) and topography (Topo) as integrated across time (T).

From the soil state equation, multiple general hypotheses can be generated and, from these, sets of working hypotheses derived. Ultimately, focused hypotheses can be constructed and tested using the leverage of the null hypothesis.

The Null Hypothesis: The Essence of Doubt

So, what is this strange device: the null hypothesis? And why would we try to disprove it? We make an observation that "the bacterium *Rhizobium leguminosarum* is the nodulating agent of peas." Perhaps we would set this up as a general hypothesis. If we rephrase this as "*Rhizobium leguminosarum* is *not* the nodulating agent of peas," then we have a null hypothesis that expresses, succinctly, our closely guarded doubts. It is the null hypothesis that we try, again and again and again, to disprove. And if we cannot disprove it, then and only then do we begin to consider that the opposite of the null hypothesis is reality. But we never abandon the null hypothesis, for a shred of evidence that supports the null hypothesis may always arise and cause us to revise our view of reality.

A seventeenth-century thinker, and sometimes called the first modern philosopher, was René Descartes. He was a prolific writer and as much as anyone is responsible for development of the scientific method (Descartes 1644). These steps are, briefly: (a) generate a hypothesis, (b) establish a null hypothesis and attempt to disprove the null hypothesis, and (c) revise the null hypothesis to accommodate observations made during the attempt to disprove. If you cannot disprove the null, then you must revise the original hypothesis. On this follows revision of the null hypothesis to accommodate observations made during the attempt to disprove. Finally, attempt to disprove the new null hypothesis. The process then starts over and theoretically continues *ad infinitum!* Descartes summarized the process in the Latin phrase *dubito ergo sum.* It is a significant misunderstanding of the scientific process, and a great disservice to those of us who do most of our work in English, that the common translation of this Latin phrase is, "I think, therefore I am!" That this is an accepted, popular translation suggests the translators either did not understand the scientific process themselves or thought that we the readers did not understand it. The phrase actually translates as, "I *doubt,* therefore I am!" (Van Doren 1991). Sure, this seems like a perplexing phrase, but it does capture the essence of science and the essence of this great philosopher's contribution to knowledge and process: that science is always based on doubt. It may be *organized doubt,* but it is still doubt.

So why might this be important in a book on pedagogy? Who could possibly care about null hypotheses, anyway, other than the white-coated scientist with her or his nose in a culture dish?

We are engaged currently in a conflict between what we think of as scientific inquiry (which is based on a foundation of *organized doubt*) and the antithesis of scientific inquiry. Scientific inquiry I conceptualize here as the process of establishing a sphere of carefully constructed precepts based on observation, null hypothesis testing, and ultimately theory establishment. These precepts guide decision making at many levels in our society, as well as make us more aware of how the universe functions. There was a trend to derive laws from these theories (for example, the law of gravity), but this trend has diminished as we have realized that knowledge is largely approximate and there are no absolutes (the law of gravity turned out to be a special, albeit important, phenomenon explained more fully under the theory of relativity, Hawking 1988).

It would be easy to label the opposite of scientific inquiry as ignorance or anti-intellectualism. This is not accurate. Here I conceptualize the antithesis of scientific inquiry as the process of establishing a sphere of carefully constructed precepts based sometimes, but not always, on usually casual observation. It does not lend itself to null hypothesis testing because information to address the question does not exist or because that information is not credible. Still, this may lead to construction of theories and often to accepted or enforced laws.

Part of the reason scientific inquiry or, more precisely, *science,* has come under such close scrutiny from the nonscience community is that we as teachers of science present hypotheses or theories as facts! When "evolution" is presented as fact, then it is in direct conflict with "intelligent design." These two camps are outwardly in direct conflict—especially when evolution is presented as fact. As fact, evolution demands proof! So how might this be resolved?

The resolution lies in that shadowy, smelly substance we call "doubt." "Evolution is the mechanism whereby organisms adapt to a continuously changing environment" is a hypothesis that we can present in the classroom. We need to recognize that we can never prove this hypothesis, but we can attempt to disprove the null hypothesis that "evolution is *not* the mechanism whereby organisms adapt to a continuously changing environment." Likewise, if put to the test, we can attempt to disprove the null hypothesis that "intelligent design is *not* the mechanism whereby organisms adapt to a continuously changing environment." In the classroom, in the laboratory, and in the field, we can design experiments to attempt to disprove these two null hypotheses, and in the process we keep an open mind as a teacher, we demonstrate the power of doubt, and we give both sides of this, or any other argument, due process.

Brilliance Among Doubters

The ravaged field grows wet with dew.

(From J. Kenyon's "Twilight: After Haying," 1996)

Years ago I was part of a team of faculty that interviewed a group of students, all of whom were applying for the prestigious Rhodes Scholarship. We interviewed these students one at a time and certainly asked a lot of questions, but mostly listened as students demonstrated their thinking skills and expressed their hopes for the future. One student I remember well because of his clear explanations and intellectually checked but otherwise unbridled enthusiasm. Among other things, he explained how calculus was really a transformation of equations to essentially higher power when integrated and lower power when differentiated. He also expressed how beautiful these transformations were. Further, he said that no arenas of thought or realms of study should not be explored, dissected, and questioned. After a rather pregnant pause, however, he made an exception. The existence of God and the divinity of Christ should never be questioned.

In another case, when I was a graduate student, one of my closest study mates was a member of a conservative Christian religion that did not believe in anything short of a strict interpretation of the Bible. Still, we took numerous classes together where evolution was a central theme and contradicted the dictates of his religion. He studied alongside me, we learned about evolution together, and he nearly always did better on examinations and in classes than I did.

So how did these two people accommodate a strong interest in science and investigation while simultaneously adhering to beliefs that should put them at odds with such? Of course, I do not know their personal specifics. But many ideas that seem mutually exclusive we as humans somehow manage to accommodate simultaneously. Even in science, there are concepts that are at odds, where one set of observations supports one concept and a second set of observations supports another. A classic example of this is the wave theory of light on the one hand and the particle theory on the other (Hawking). There is good evidence to support both, but it is difficult to imagine where both models make sense simultaneously. Still, a part of the human experience is to accommodate ambiguity in most of life, including education. The challenge is to accommodate and even enjoy ambiguity and, further, to recognize when it elicits cognitive dissonance that the associated discomfort is a symptom of an impending learning opportunity. This goes for instructors as well as students.

It is clear to me that minds of even similar humans work very differently, and different humans view things differently. Nonetheless, my long-term observations suggest that if one presents the same conditions for, and data from, an experiment to reasonably intelligent individuals and ask them to draw conclusions, they will come to similar if not identical conclusions. If any individual comes to different conclusions, one should look pretty carefully at what and why they are different. In my experience, they likely have come across something well worth considering. Further, if everyone comes up with a different conclusion, then it is likely the data, conditions, or something else was faulty or ambiguous. It is also possible there are multiple conclusions and some integration of conclusions that approaches truth or makes more sense than a single individual analysis.

For several years, I have been teaching a sophomore-level course called Environment and Society. It is a discussion course directed by our readings of much classical environmental literature. As a final project, students role-play in groups and address in detail an environmental issue identified during the previous several weeks by the class membership. During a recent semester, we asked the question: How would energy development, specifically natural gas development, impact air quality? The students divided themselves into four groups: indigenous people, industrialists, environmentalists, and scientists. The focus was for each group to take and develop a position on the question and defend that position. Each group was allowed considerable time to prepare and orally present their findings and position in class. The groups were allowed to question and challenge each of the other groups.

Much had preceded this final exercise, including reading and discussion of hypothesis testing and use of the null hypothesis to address complex problems. It was amazing how quickly students discarded the tenets of the null hypothesis and found themselves asking for and, on the other side, trying to provide proofs to support their position. The industrialists realized the power they had to demand that others prove that energy development was increasing air pollution. None of the other three groups were able to counter this strategic move, mainly because they did not have the experience or confidence to state that proof was impossible, especially in an atmosphere where they challenged a system replete with resources and an entrenched status quo.

I have since contemplated why the class in general failed to use the tools for analysis we had painstakingly developed together. My sense is that use of the null hypothesis is not intuitively obvious to most people, and to use it takes practice. I also tend to overexplain things for students and not give readers or listeners a chance to develop their own version of things or take them to a depth consistent with their own needs, desires, or abilities.

In the future, I will give students more practice using the null hypothesis, and I will reduce it to the basic essentials, especially for use in the undergraduate classroom. I can imagine myself lecturing to a class: "Organized doubt, since you can never prove, you must disprove. So establish your hypothesis and a null hypothesis, and devise tests or strategies to disprove that null hypothesis, and if you fail to disprove…." And as the apparent double-talk swirls bafflingly around them, I will start to see eyes glaze over. From the back row will come deep breathing.

And thus will go the class—down an avenue of boredom at best and confusion likely. Hopefully there is something better.

A Final Observation

"So Rob," say I, "what makes you suspicious of evolution as a mechanism where survival of the fittest has resulted though time in increasingly complex organisms?"

"Well," says he, "it is hard for me to imagine generation of organisms of such complexity and variety via merely random events stimulated by a changing environment. I think there must be a master planner or master plan out there somewhere."

I respond, "So can you put your idea into a hypothesis, Rob?"

"Sure. There is an intelligent designer that is responsible for creation of the Earth and its inhabitants as we see it today," says Rob.

"Would you mind if I restated that hypothesis?"

"What do you have in mind?"

"Well, I suspect that you could not prove to my or anyone else's satisfaction the validity of your hypothesis. However, try this: 'There is *not* an intelligent designer that is responsible for creation of the Earth,'" say I.

"I fail to understand where this is going," says Rob.

"Rob, I have merely restated your hypothesis."

I write it on the chalkboard.

"If you can disprove this statement, this null hypothesis, then such helps to validate your hypothesis. Take your time on this, but remember here we seek our own tests, data, and observations, and we seek certified tests, data, and observations of others in this exercise."

"Okay, but don't different cultures, even within our own American culture, have different acceptable tests, data, observations, and even certifications?" Rob says adroitly.

"Oh, my," say I. "You are subtly yet distinctly changing the rules, Rob."

References

Campbell, N.A., and J.B. Reece. 2005. *Biology*, 7th ed. San Francisco: Benjamin Cummings.

Chamberlin, T.C. 1890. The method of multiple working hypotheses. Reprinted in 1965, *Science* 148:754–59.

Crick, F.H.C. 1962. The genetic code. *Scientific American* (October) 207:66–77.

Descartes, R. 1644. *Principia philosophiae*. Latin text published by Elzevir of Amsterdam. Also published in 1647 in French by LeGras of Paris. Numerous translations are available, including the one used here: Cottingham, J., R. Stoothoff, and D. Murdoch, trans., 1985. Principles of philosophy. In *The philosophical writings of Descartes*, vol. 1, 177–291, paperback. Cambridge, UK: Cambridge University Press.

Eliot, T.S. 1919. The love song of J. Alfred Prufrock. www.wsu.edu: 8080/~wldciv/world_civ_reader/world_civ_reader_2/eliot.html.

Freeman, S. 2005. *Biological science*, 2nd ed. Boston: Pearson Prentice Hall.

Grebstein, S.N., ed. 1960. *Monkey trial: The state of Tennessee vs. John Thomas Scopes*. Boston: Houghton Mifflin Company.

Hardin, G. 1968. The tragedy of the commons. *Science* 162:1243–48.

Hawking, S.W. 1988. *A brief history of time*. New York: Bantam Books.

Jenny, H. 1941. *Factors of soil formation: A system of quantitative pedology.* New York: McGraw-Hill.

Kenyon, J. 1996. Twilight: After haying. In *Otherwise: New and selected poems.* St. Paul, MN: Graywolf Press. Also reprinted in Keillor, G., ed. 2002. *Good poems.* New York: Penguin Group, 411–12.

Kornberg, A. 1962. *Enzymatic synthesis of DNA.* New York: John Wiley & Sons.

Plato. Ca. 385 BC. *The republic.* See Book VII. Several translations available. The one used here was translated by Bloom, A. 1978. *The republic of Plato.* 2nd ed., paperback. New York: Basic Books. *Myth of the cave:* see 514a to 517b. Socrates question to Thrasymachus, see 338c.

Raven, P.H., G.B. Johnson, J.B. Losos, and S.R. Singer. 2005. *Biology,* 7th ed. New York: McGraw-Hill.

Van Doren, C. 1991. *A history of knowledge: Past, present, and future.* New York: Ballantine Books.

Watson, J.D. 1968. *The double helix.* New York: Penguin Group, New American Library.

Watson, J.D., and F.H.C. Crick. 1953. The structure of DNA. *Cold Spring Harbor Symposium on Quantitative Biology* 18:123.

Weisz, P.B. 1963. *The science of biology.* New York: McGraw-Hill.

Wells, H.G., J.S. Huxley, and G.P. Wells. 1929. *The science of life.* 1934 printing, Country Life Press. New York: Literary Guild.

Williams, S.E. 1997. Tangled. *Rangelands* 19:39.

5

James K. Wangberg

James Wangberg has been the associate dean for academic and student programs in the University of Wyoming College of Agriculture since 1999 and is a professor of entomology. He graduated from Humboldt State University in California with B.A. and M.A. degrees in biology and earned his Ph.D. in entomology from the University of Idaho. His teaching career began in 1975 at Texas Tech University, where he advanced to chair, Department of Entomology, and was later named director, Texas Tech University Center, Junction. He came to UW in 1986 to head the Department of Plant Science. In 1993 he was selected as the founding director for the University of Wyoming's Center for Teaching Excellence.

Wangberg's research has included the biology, behavior, and ecology of insects associated with western United States native plants with an emphasis on gall insects. Additional studies have included the ecology of fire ants and the biology of aquatic insects. Long-term interests have been teaching, advising, and faculty and student development. He has received several university, regional, and national teaching and advising awards.

Professor Wangberg is a member of numerous national, regional, and local professional associations and committees, including the Entomological Society of America and the Academic Programs Section of the National Association of State Universities and Land Grant Colleges. He was the founding contributing editor for an educational column in the *American Entomologist,* the flagship journal for the Entomological Society of America, and author and presenter of more than two hundred scientific articles, reports, and abstracts; invitational papers; and seminars. He has written and edited three other books, the most recent being the entertaining educational account of insect romance, *Six-Legged Sex: The Erotic Lives of Bugs* (2001, Fulcrum Publishing). His books and seminars have led to numerous television and radio appearances, interviews, and features, including the nationally syndicated game show *To Tell the Truth;* Paul Harvey's *News and Comment; the Tom Snyder Show; Kid's News;* and several local or regional news and entertainment programs.

The Teachings of Bugs and Slugs: Unexpected Lessons

On the first part of the journey
I was looking at all the life
There were plants and birds and rocks and things
There was sand and hills and rings
The first thing I met was a fly with a buzz
And the sky with no clouds
The heat was hot and the ground was dry
But the air was full of sound

(Song lyrics from Dewey Bunnell's "A Horse with No Name")

Many metaphors have been proposed for teachers, but one that has always appealed to me is the *outdoor adventure guide*. Learning is like an adventure safari, requiring a skilled guide to navigate unfamiliar territories and to aid in the discovery of new things. Surprises are often encountered on the journey, resulting in unexpected lessons. Perhaps the metaphor resonates strongly with me because as a student and as a teacher, learning has often occurred in the field, only a small imaginative leap away from an actual foreign safari. My early passion for natural history and subsequent career as a field-oriented insect biologist makes the analogy natural. I have often felt as if I were on an insect safari in search of some new species to either bag with my net or to observe and later report for the first time on its exotic behaviors. The love of nature's wonders was ingrained in me as a child, and the opportunities for field study as a student and teacher have persisted throughout my life. No wonder I always loved the day our class went on a field trip, and no wonder I have employed field trips in my teaching throughout a more than thirty-year university career.

As a student, I preferred a field trip to sitting in a classroom and taking notes or, worse yet, taking a quiz or an exam. I am sure that many of my peers viewed it as a day off, something like our earlier experiences in junior high or high school when we got to see a film—just sit back, watch the movie, don't take notes. The announcement of a field trip elicited the same reaction—just get on the bus, see some sights, and spend time with friends. But a funny thing often happened on these field trips. Sometimes we learned things. And sometimes *what* we learned was more unexpected than having learned at all.

Slugs, Bugs, and Morality

One of my earliest recollections of a surprise field trip experience involved a giant slug. The unexpected lesson occurred in my freshman year at Humboldt State University, at that time one of the small liberal arts colleges in the California state college system, located on the northern coast overlooking the Pacific Ocean and with the dramatic backdrop of a redwood forest. The lesson I learned that day was one I would need to reprise twenty-one years later in a university class of my own in Texas.

I am certain the professor who led our introductory botany class on the first field trip of the semester had not planned to talk about banana slugs. Nor did we, his students, expect more than a nature hike through a coastal redwood forest with stops to identify indigenous plant species, species I would later learn to name—assorted mosses, ferns, fungi, and liverworts. The field trip curriculum changed dramatically when a classmate, seeing a giant banana slug stretched out on the trunk of a redwood, gleefully pulled out a large knife and sliced the creature in half. Not many people care much for eight-inch yellow-bodied slugs and their slime trails, and few would mourn this creature's death, but Professor Smith was outraged over the cruel act. The knife-wielding student received a passionate tongue-lashing about respecting nature and all living things. In the process, the entire class got a one-minute lesson on the ethos of studying nature and science. The offending student was completely taken by surprise, as were the rest of us, but everyone got the message. Some were probably more impacted by Professor Smith's discourse than others, but that single episode was the talk of the class at the end of the day. I don't know how many others would recall that incident as vividly as I do today, but if I was the only one of those twenty-four students with the indelible lesson learned, the lesson was not wasted.

It would be a lesson repeated twenty-one years later when I found my own entomology students torturing some insects during a two-week field course. Six-legged creatures apparently don't garner any more compassion than slugs by most college students, at least judging by the behavior of a small group of students collecting insects one evening. The students had gathered at a favorite collecting site on the Texas Tech University Center, Junction (TTUCJ) campus. The campus, located in the Texas Hill Country renowned for breathtaking spring wildflowers and scenery, was an idyllic summer camp setting for a variety of field-oriented science classes, including my course, Insect Natural History. Every evening my students and I would spend considerable time stationed at a black light trap, an apparatus that resembled an old screened telephone booth with specialized lamps on top, emitting beacons of ultraviolet light that are highly attractive to many night-flying insects. Two of the more spectacular and common insects were victimized that evening. The hummingbird moth, characterized by its hummingbird-like appearance in flight, has a long, coiled feeding tube for gathering nectar from blossoms in the same fashion as its namesake. A couple of students were having fun at this creature's expense by enticing another large insect, a caterpillar hunter (a beetle with large, powerful jaws), to bite the moth's feeding tube, stretching it its full length and then ripping it from the head.

My outrage was no less than Professor Smith's two decades earlier. A professional educator still in command of his emotions would have recognized this as a "teachable moment," but I was too angry and disappointed to teach without passion. My sermon to those students was also about the ethos of studying living things and respecting the objects of our science. The students were completely surprised by my reaction and confused by the notion that these bugs somehow had rights that I was defending.

Needless to say, no other insects were tortured during that field course, but the lesson did more than just curtail abusing some living creatures. In the coming days, the students displayed a respect for the insects and habitats that we studied, and by the end of the course there was mutual respect for one another and the journey we had taken together. It had not been a planned lesson in my curriculum, but my philosophy of biology and how to interact with the objects of our study is now a regular part of what I teach on the first day of class. The ethos and morality of science was first taught to me as an 18-year-old freshman and is now routinely passed on to other students, without waiting for further incidents to trigger the lecture.

My hope is that students come away with a greater level of respect for the natural world. Perhaps Professor Smith does not recall the day as I do, and if he does I doubt that he knew the power of what was taught that day. I may not recall all the fundamentals of botany that he lectured on for the rest of the semester, but I benefited greatly by being in that class.

Just a Day at the Beach

Other field trips at Humboldt State left lasting impressions of a different kind, and again I hope I have instilled them in student participants during field trips I have organized. There were good reasons for biology majors studying in a coastal environment to have frequent field trips to the beach. We spent much time exploring tide pools, primarily identifying their rich array of animal life. The class moved over the tidal flats like a grazing herd, but we were selective in our grazing habits, either stopping to examine and collect creatures whose names were on the instructor's list or restricting our search and attention to the specific animal group for the week, like the various species of sea stars, sea urchins, sea cucumbers, and other echinoderms. Whatever the learning menu, we welcomed the chance to wade in the surf and smell the salt air of the northern California coast.

At the time I thought I was learning about the biology and ecology of intertidal organisms, and in fact I learned quite a bit over the course of my entire biology curriculum. What stayed with me longer than the scientific names and principles was an appreciation for a particular place and habitat. In retrospect, it was the equivalent of the music appreciation class that I *had to take*. At the time, I had no appreciation of classical music, but I could regurgitate enough facts on an exam to earn a "B" in the course. Thirty years later, an appreciation for classical music emerged as if it had always been with me, like a smoldering ember, but now fanned by a gust, igniting into flame. That flame is still being fueled by some memories of my music appreciation class. Conversely, I could have told you at the time I was on the biology field trip that I was enjoying myself, learning some things, and knowing that this knowledge was providing the foundation I needed for future studies of natural science. I already appreciated science. That ember had ignited as a boy. Unbeknownst to me was another ember that started growing on those field trips: the introduction to a habitat and to ways of learning about the new habitat. To this day I can look out over an intertidal zone and begin to picture the complexity of life below me. If

I walk back onto those tidal flats, I resume where I left off in 1969, look-ing for creatures, assigning names to some, wondering about others, and experiencing the joy of learning. I can appreciate the web of life that oc-cupies that space and draw solace in knowing that the plants and animals I once touched or collected are still there, as are the biological processes that sustain their populations and drive their evolution. Those field trip experiences gave me an invaluable gift: an ability to return and continue what began decades ago.

I have accumulated many such gifts from my field experiences as a student and as a teacher. Today I drive across the Wyoming plains, looking over the expanse of grass and sage. So many people traveling the same highway see miles and miles of sagebrush and little else, sometimes refer-ring to it as a moonscape or an empty desert. Because of the gift of field work in Wyoming and Idaho, I see much more. I can see the tiny ground-nesting leaf-cutter bee because of the time I spent observing and noting its behavior in a secluded corner of the Snake River Basin. I can see the rattlesnake coiled in the shade of a winterfat shrub because of a previous chance encounter. I can see thousands of insect galls on rabbitbrush, big sagebrush, and other native range plants because of the years of graduate research and hours examining their contents. I can see the harvester ants trailing away from their barren mounds in search of seeds, and I can see the dung beetle, the ground beetle, and the stink beetle sharing their neighborhood. When I look out across the wide expanse of prairie, I can see life in the air, on the plants, on the soil surface, and underground. The teachers who introduced me to such places gave me the gift of sight.

The Junction Experience

The unhappy insect torture episode at the Texas Tech University Center, Junction (TTUCJ) was an aberration in an otherwise fabulous teaching and learning setting. The TTUCJ may be better known for its historical place in the life of former Texas A&M University (TAMU) foot-ball coach Paul "Bear" Bryant depicted in the Hollywood film *The Junction Boys*. This place has impacted far more TTU students and faculty than the handful of TAMU football camp survivors.

After Texas Tech University acquired the campus, it put its own trade-mark on it: "The Junction Experience." This place became the site for my best teaching experience and my students' best learning experience in my first eleven years as a professor.[*] The Junction Experience is unique for its communal living arrangements and summer camp setting, which fosters a community of teachers and students around the dining hall table, at the picnic grounds or campfire at night, or on the athletic fields. Students and teachers worked, lived, and played together for a fifteen-day period. Building a community of learners and focusing on the coursework came naturally. If it didn't come about naturally, it happened because the students were residents of that 410-acre campus for fifteen days, whether they liked it or not.

The Junction Experience also smoothed the transitions from lecture to laboratory and field. Boundaries among these three course components blurred because it was easy to cancel a lecture to take advantage of some natural phenomenon that might be occurring right outside the door, such as a column of army ants marching across the field, a temporary phenomenon worthy of any entomology class's attention. Sometimes a student's discovery of a new insect or an important microhabitat prompted us to go on an impromptu field trip. One day's topic changed from aquatic insects to parasitic insects on mammals because the mammalogy class meeting next door had collected some Mexican free-tailed bats the previous night and the bats were loaded with parasitic insects rarely seen by beginning entomology students. The campus was like a biological field station, perfectly situated to teach and learn entomology. The field was our laboratory, and the classroom was base camp. Natural occurrences outside could dictate the day's activity, and students could determine what was of greatest interest by being good observers. As the teacher, I knew that I could often lecture on a topic and, rather than rely on visual aids, could take the class outside to show them firsthand what was discussed in that day's lecture. The spontaneous and improvisational nature of the Junction Experience added significant value to our teaching and learning.

These opportunities are not afforded by the typical classrooms assigned for teaching on main campuses. My personal challenge has been to

---

[*] I was inspired to write an educational article about this professional period, titled "The Junction experience: My best teaching experience and my students' best learning experience," *American Entomologist*, 1994, 40(3):136–37.

recreate some of the qualities of the Junction campus and, like a jazz musician, embrace improvisation. Easier said than done. As counterintuitive as it may sound, improvisation for me requires excellent planning, organization, and knowledge of the subject. Only with the security of knowing my subject, planning how one topic flows to the next, and keeping the big picture or course theme in mind can I deviate from a planned lecture to take full advantage of a student's question, a current event that relates to the course, or the surprise of an interesting insect walking across the classroom floor, capturing everyone's curiosity. I welcome these classroom surprises.

The laboratory can be a good substitute for the field experience. In entomology classes, we resurrect the insect species encountered on a field trip by bringing out museum trays of pinned insect specimens or vials with insects preserved in alcohol. Clearly this is no match for the living thing interacting with its natural surroundings, but examining specimens in labs has the advantage of close inspection with microscopes to appreciate the anatomical characteristics and to compare and contrast related insect groups. Dead insects hold still for inspection and never run or fly off before we have seen everything we need to see. The laboratory can be a home for living insects, too. Some insects, like cockroaches, are the entomologist's equivalent to the white rat, a perfect experimental insect for studies in anatomy, physiology, and behavior. My entomology labs have brought a little bit of the field indoors with observational bee hives mounted in the windows. A bee colony with queen, drones, and worker bees safely secured between two glass panels and positioned for easy viewing may not be the same as discovering a hive in nature, but it certainly affords students the chance to comfortably view honey bees at work in a hive with no fear of stings. My labs have housed terrariums and aquariums to hold a variety of terrestrial and aquatic insects that have been reared in the lab or collected on some earlier class field trip. If we can't go outside, it's always possible to bring a little of the outdoors into the classroom.

The Junction Experience taught me to organize laboratory exercises in ways that might mimic the natural outdoor environment. For example, one of my teaching experiments at the University of Wyoming was to design a laboratory exercise that was something like a brain teaser—a puzzle for students to match various kinds of insects with certain objects. Objects might be a piece of wood or a leaf with some characteristic type of insect damage, an insect artifact (nest), an insect gall, or fruit with feeding scars. I wanted to challenge students with the tasks of matching a wide array of insects with insect-related objects. By logic and the process of elimination, students would have to relate insect size, modes of locomotion, types of mouthpart modifications for feeding, and a host of other characteristics they were learning in order to make the correct associations. My goal was to create a brain teaser and real puzzle, the entomological equivalent of Sudoku. For individuals who enjoy puzzles, the exercise was fun and manageable. For others who preferred information presented in clear and organized ways, the exercise was too messy, challenging, and sometimes frustrating. For those less able to cope with such ambiguity, teamwork and cooperation helped. The old adage of two heads being better than one was often the key for students to successfully complete this simulation of nature's confusing picture.

Because of the Junction Experience, I prefer to either lecture in the laboratory or schedule my lecture classroom adjacent to the lab so the students and I can easily move from one setting to the other and literally put our hands on some material or view actual specimens. I welcome opportunities to have students engaged in their learning, moving around, talking with each other, and solving problems and puzzles. Anything that blurs the boundaries and facilitates transitioning from one kind of learning activity to another is my preferred teaching style, a style that had its genesis in the field.

Insect Safaris and Scavenger Hunts

The Junction Experience also inspired my ideas for an insect scavenger hunt and insect safari, activities that would later be incorporated into courses at the University of Wyoming. Making insect collections has been a mainstay in introductory entomology courses in universities nationwide. They serve several important learning objectives. Making a collection familiarizes students with some standard entomological and scientific techniques. Collecting insects introduces students to the habitats of insects and provides the richer context of knowing where insects live, what they eat, and how they behave. Central to insect collecting is insect identification by proper scientific name within an understood scientific hierarchy. By collecting insects, students learn to classify insects in relation to all other living things.

Being true to my favorite teaching metaphor, I began to call insect-collecting field trips "insect safaris." Why not add a touch of hyperbole and bring a sense of adventure to the notion of chasing six-legged creatures with a net? For the uninitiated, insect collecting actually can be quite an adventure. I have seen more than one student fall in a stream or beaver pond in an attempt to capture a new insect prize. The adventure may involve animals other than insects: snakes, skunks, porcupines, and mother cows, for instance. Insect collecting is not for the squeamish, either, as veteran collectors will testify. The adventure includes careful picking through cow manure and roadkill for those special insect species that prefer to live and dine in feces and rotting flesh. Even the beginning collector can become quite maniacal about exploring these habitats. Many a time I have piloted a fifteen-passenger university van filled with entomology students, who ordered me to stop upon sight of a carcass by the side of the road. It must have looked like a piñata, the van bursting open and students spilling onto the roadside with forceps, alcohol vials, and nets, eager to capture their prey from the grisly habitat. Such enthusiasm! Such memories.

Former students frequently recall how much fun they had and how much they learned. One University of Wyoming entomology course developed by colleagues specifically for teachers, titled Insects for Teachers, featured the insect collection as the principal student project. I joined the team of instructors and helped lead several insect safaris to the local Medicine Bow National Forest. Our insect safaris were often structured like a scavenger hunt. Each student was given an insect scavenger hunt list and challenged to collect as many of the items from the list as possible in the time allotted. The list was strategically crafted to expose students to different groups of insects, different insect habitats, different collecting techniques, and a variety of what you might call insect trivia, for example, an insect with a syringe for a mouth, an insect with color patterns on its wings, an insect that feeds on other insects, and so forth. Our field and collecting experiences were not unlike those I have already described. Every student had a chance to explore new environments and discover new things. Each brought personal treasures back to the lab for closer inspection or for sharing with others. Their enthusiasm during the course was contagious, but what has most impressed me about those teachers is the consistent positive feedback we receive from them years later. Recently I encountered a former Insects for Teachers student, a teacher who took the course in the 1980s. She enthusiastically recalled the course and related to me about how much she had learned, but most importantly, she wanted me to hear these words, uttered with great pride: "And I still have my insect collection!"

The Desert Field Trip

A sense of community develops in classes where students are actively engaged in their learning and working together. I first became part of such a community when I enrolled as a senior in a biology seminar that culminated in a ten-day spring-break field trip to the Mojave and Sonoran deserts of southern California and Arizona. The desert field-trip class, as it was generally called, taught me the requisite elements of the biology and ecology of another ecosystem, but like the field trips to the beach, there were greater lessons learned that would shape my teaching.

Enrollment was limited to fifteen undergraduate seniors and master's–level graduate students, and a sixteenth student if licensed to drive a school bus, the planned mode of transportation for the extended field trip. Class met a couple of hours a week to hear lectures, review and discuss readings, and cover important aspects of desert ecosystems in anticipation of the spring break trip. Critical to a successful field experience was the assignment of specific topics to each student. Each of us was to become the resident expert on some aspect of desert ecology, the "go-to person" on the field trip when questions arose about the subject. There was a herpetology expert, the student who was to be the principal resource on all matters concerning desert lizards, snakes, and tortoises. There were an insect expert, a bird expert, a mammal expert, and several students assigned as plant experts, dividing their duties among cacti, grasses, and myriad other flowering plants. There were also assignments for the experts on geology, climatology, and geography. Being designated as the insect or snake specialist did not excuse you from learning about all of the other areas; it simply placed you in the lead role as desert insect or snake guide and key resource for others when questions arose about such creatures encountered on the trip. Each student also had the responsibility for presenting a formal class seminar on their assigned subject before the trip.

The course proved to be an exceptional model for teaching and learning. Dividing the class subjects among student experts created what professional educators define as a learning community, and what a community it was! We learned from one another, and we learned our subject well because there is no better way to learn the subject than by having to teach it yourself. The student was the teacher and the teacher was the student, which is precisely the way I like to find myself in classes that I teach today.

Throughout the trip, the flowering-plant experts were especially busy, because at each scheduled or unscheduled stop, there were typically several unknown flowers to identify. Long after the bus departed the site, flower specimens circulated among the passengers, each person with field guides and plant keys, enthusiastically trying to identify the mystery plant species. It seemed amazing to me how excited some students could become over a tiny yellow flower, but some of them were probably amazed or amused at others' passion for insects and desert tarantulas.

This approach to teaching and learning placed special responsibilities on the students and in so doing validated their contributions. It helped build self-esteem and mutual respect for one another. We learned about collaboration, cooperation, and team building, in part from the academic assignment but in even larger part from the time spent traveling together, setting up camps each night, sharing camp duties, and functioning as a family. We learned about each other and developed an appreciation for our commonalities and for our differences. It was a lesson in human diversity.

What else did I learn? I learned to drive a school bus and obtained a commercial-class driving permit, and also learned that school buses are not well designed to traverse deep desert sand washes or navigate narrow, twisting roads. I learned that it takes fifteen college students to chase down, surround, and capture one zebra-tailed lizard in 105-degree heat. I learned emergency first aid and that long hair can be used in place of sutures to close a head wound. I learned of life underground. I learned how to track a desert bighorn sheep. I learned the touch of a kangaroo rat's feet on my face and the tracks of a sidewinder rattlesnake where I slept. I learned that I wanted to learn much more.

Conclusions

A joy of learning was one of the most important outcomes from these experiences. Reflecting on my field trips as a student and teacher brings awareness and appreciation of the many unexpected lessons learned, lessons that were not part of the course syllabus or part of the planned class activity. Nonetheless they were lessons that influenced me professionally, informed my approach to teaching, and shaped my teaching philosophy. The joy of learning about insects, the ecology of deserts and seashores, and plants and animals, was certainly what any student or teacher would welcome, but rarely do we articulate that as a goal. More typical are goals that relate to absorbing subject-matter content and scientific or technical skills. But the greater skill is the ability to ask questions, study, and learn for a lifetime, all of which were fostered by the memorable times as a student and teacher in the field.

The other unexpected lesson that accompanied discovery and engagement in learning was the value of community. These experiences taught a respect for others and a greater appreciation and respect for diversity—diverse personalities, diverse ideas, diverse backgrounds. While I thought I was engaged in studies of plants and animals, I was often learning more about myself and other people. Being engaged in a learning community is a life lesson for engagement in larger communities and within society.

Lastly, the teachings of bugs and slugs resulted in a stronger sense of self. There are continued lessons about values—the values of knowledge and education, the values of ethics and morality, the values of relationships and of life. My sense of self grew to become less about me and more about connections with others and with the environment. I continue to learn, and there continue to be unexpected lessons.

6

Sonya S. Meyer

Sonya Meyer joined the University of Wyoming's Department of Family and Consumer Sciences faculty in 1986. Meyer is an associate professor teaching in the textiles and merchandising option. Her scholarship combines her love of historic costume with design, creating one-of-a-kind fiber-art dolls. She and her program colleagues are committed to developing in students a greater global awareness, leading to an increase in socially responsible and sustainable apparel and design industries. Prior to her arrival at Wyoming, Meyer was on the faculty at Washburn University in Topeka, Kansas. Meyer received her B.S.E. in home economics education from Emporia State University in Emporia, Kansas. Both her M.S. and Ph.D. are in adult education from Kansas State University. Before joining the ranks of higher education faculty, Meyer taught home economics at the secondary level in Dodge City, Kansas. It is there that she started her study tour experience, coordinating field trips to Denver and Kansas City for her students. Also, during her tenure with Dodge City Senior High, she had her first taste of international travel with students. She served as faculty sponsor one summer for the high school's European study tour, and she hasn't stopped since.

The World Is My Classroom

Just what is a loo anyway?
Tell me again how to ask for directions in Italian.

Travel in a foreign land provides a faculty member the opportunity to know students on an entirely different level than in a traditional classroom setting. I consider myself very fortunate to have shared travel experiences and adventures with students for the past several years through my department's study-abroad short-course program. A short course is generally considered to be of limited duration, approximately one to four weeks. The study-abroad program I conduct relates to the textile and apparel industry and has been offered for between one and three credit hours. The number of credits has been determined by the length of the study abroad plus predeparture meetings. Two study tours have been interdisciplinary in nature, combining art history with fashion and textile studies. Our study tours have included travel to Great Britain and Italy.

Through our travel adventures, I have observed our students in action, allowing them to apply the discipline-based knowledge gained in the classroom, exercise their critical-thinking and problem-solving skills, and practice their professional skills and behavior, while helping them recognize the importance of continuing to learn and discover new information. Observing the students in action in a foreign land and recognizing the growth occurring is one thing. Trying to put it into a formal assessment of learning is something else.

I believe I can assess these changes through the writing the students complete to receive credit for the tour. The students must write a formal paper on a company, institution, designer, or art piece that they have researched prior to departure. They keep a daily journal of their activities, both scheduled and unscheduled, throughout the duration of the study tour. Listening to students' conversations and watching their behavior creates another opportunity to assess the program's impact. There is also something to be said for just "knowing that you know." Other faculty, at both the University of Wyoming and other institutions across the country, generally refer to this as observing the "ah-ha" moments. It is a highlight for me to watch for and recognize the "ah-ha" moments when they occur;

generally the students' faces brighten with a look of wonder as they connect the experience with something learned in an on-campus class.

Many of the students with whom I have traveled over the past several
years were eager and open to learn all they could about the countries, institutions, and businesses visited. The students became active participants
in the learning process, and they embraced the experiences. They often
used scheduled free time to discover more about the cities or countries
visited. What follows is a synopsis of my observations and stories collected
throughout the various study-abroad courses during my tenure at the
University of Wyoming. I do not name names to protect the innocent or,
in some cases, the not-so-innocent.

So, Are You Crazy?

I have often been asked by colleagues why I choose to offer study-
abroad courses. Some of them have actually been kind enough to not call
me crazy to my face. After all, the planning for the next study tour starts
shortly after returning home from the one just completed. It takes an attention to detail and at times the patience of a saint, which I do not have.
It involves a great deal of communication with the European travel agent,
working with the campus Office of International Programs, marketing the
next study tour, meeting with students, and answering question after question after question.

I do it because I love travel and introducing students to new cultures
and ideas. This is not an uncommon teaching tool. Many faculty incorporate the concept of field trips into their regular course curriculum so students can observe course content put into action. The study tour extends
that technique beyond the duration of the course. Specifically, our study
tours offer students the opportunity to visit fashion designer showrooms,
textile manufacturers, museums, and historic and cultural sites. Even
though the study tours are short in duration, generally ten days to two
weeks, the participants are introduced to cultures other than their own.

Many believe that short-term study-abroad programs are not as effective as the longer term offerings. However, Tammy L. Lewis and Richard A.
Niesenbaum, authors of "The Benefits of Short-Term Study Abroad" (*The
Chronicle of Higher Education,* June 3, 2005, sec. B), found that their short-
term offering to Costa Rica resulted in a positive global influence on the

student participants. Because their course is interdisciplinary in nature, students were more willing to take course work outside of their major when returning to campus and demonstrated an increased interest in interdisciplinary studies. More importantly for study abroad, though, was that the participants continued travel or study-abroad activities. Additionally, Lewis and Niesenbaum's students felt their participation had influenced their perceptions of the costs and benefits of globalization.

The participants in the short courses I have offered echo Lewis and Niesenbaum's students. Many have voiced their desire to return to the country visited or to travel to other countries once they have experienced travel outside of the United States and developed self-confidence in their ability to navigate in a strange city. Even though students in our program are required to take a course titled Textiles in the Global Marketplace, globalization of the industry becomes even more apparent to students who participate in the study tours. The world does seem a much smaller place to many students once they have had this travel opportunity.

Traveling abroad offers an additional advantage, especially in the textile and apparel industry and art history. Today's textile industry is indeed global in nature. Manufacturers are found worldwide, and country borders have disappeared among the top fashion designers. Introducing students to some of the designer workrooms and manufacturing facilities brings this fact home to them in a way that a textbook cannot.

Jean Schaefer, former UW art department chairwoman, was the co–faculty coordinator on the two interdisciplinary study tours. She summed up what many faculty believe about the advantages of study-abroad programs, no matter the length. She included the following to her syllabus for the one-credit art course for the May 2003 London Study Tour: "To travel is to see objects face-to-face. No amount of 'book learning' can take the place of the direct experience of a work of art." I believe Jean's statement can be true about any subject, not just art. When students see face-to-face the machinery in operation in a textile mill or interact with a designer or see a painting hanging in a gallery that up to this point was only an image in a textbook, then learning comes to life in a meaningful way.

What is good for the student is also good for the faculty member. A number of colleagues, both at UW as well as other institutions around the

country, feel that providing these opportunities for our students also creates greater cultural awareness and tolerance. The faculty also appreciate
being able to see firsthand new techniques, designs, or a piece of art that
before had only been witnessed in a textbook. It provides us with information we can bring back to campus to share with students unable to participate in the study-tour program. In fact, one of the highlights for many on
the 2005 Italy tour was a visit to the Swarovski crystal offices in Milan. It was
probably one of the best industry visits of any of the international tours I
have taken.

This appointment provided students the opportunity to meet and interact with Swarovski's Milan directors of design and marketing. These individuals shared new trends and designs for Swarovski crystals' use in home interiors, such as crystal bath faucet knobs, and apparel embellishment in the
next year or season. Students were able to leaf through Swarovski's design
trend books, an opportunity that consumers (tourists or not) rarely experience. Trend books are shared with designers and their firms as a method of
marketing the company's new designs for home interiors and apparel embellishment. It was exciting for all of us to view these books and samples.

The students had an opportunity to see these new trends firsthand,
and I had an opportunity to assess the students' professional skills and
behavior. The students were not only allowed but also encouraged to ask
questions of our two hosts. Their questions were well put and knowledge
based. "What is the time frame for a new design, from idea to appearing
in the books?" "Could you share with us some of the current designers
using or planning to use crystals this next season?" "What is the advantage
of creating a light fixture with crystals?" A stimulating discussion followed.
The students conducted themselves as if in a business meeting. The two
directors were impressed by the students' knowledge and enthusiasm for
not only the product but also design in general.

The visit to Swarovski inspired students in the creation of their own
design and art projects upon returning to campus. Maybe their designs
did not include crystals, but the inspiration of possibilities was evident.
What they saw during that visit helped them to see "outside the box" with
their own creations. Several of the students mentioned that even the meeting room was an inspiration to them. "Did you see *that* light fixture? Who

makes a light fixture with crystals? And the displays. Wow, crystals on jeans, sweet!" Yes, the lighting in the room was a bit different, and we noticed the difference upon entering the room. Our hosts explained the use of the crystals in helping to reflect and disperse the light throughout the room. We did get to see crystal bling used to decorate a pair of blue jeans even before they were on the market here in the United States.

The appointment opened their eyes and minds not only to their own design projects but also to the possibilities for their future. The willingness of the directors to share their stories and their work helped these students expand their professional goals. Many were struck with the possibilities awaiting them after graduation. Honestly I think the students' eyes were shining brighter than any of Swarovski's crystals, they were that inspired by the visit.

Do They Really Learn Anything?

An exciting bonus of study-abroad courses is the opportunity for faculty to interact with students. Traveling with students is rewarding for several reasons. One of the most valuable is witnessing how students deal with challenges in unfamiliar territory. In the classroom, it is not always apparent that students are competent critical thinkers. Place them in an unfamiliar city with an unfamiliar language and ask them to find their way to their next scheduled appointment, and they demonstrate competence in a way not generally seen in the traditional classroom.

When possible, our study tours begin with a guided tour of the city in which we are staying. This allows the students to become somewhat acquainted with their surroundings, and they are often introduced to some of the city's history and culture. I have also found this helps to ease the jet lag experienced by most of the group. Upon arrival and check-in to our hotel, the students receive maps of the city and updated itineraries with general directions on how to reach the scheduled appointments. At this time the group also receives their individual public-transportation passes. For example, while in London we receive passes that we are able to use on the Tube or city buses. In Florence, Italy, however, we do not receive public-transportation passes as most of our scheduled appointments are within a comfortable walking distance from our hotel or are located outside of the city limits, where we are bused to our appointments.

Other than the official scheduled tour of the city, there are no other scheduled appointments for the first day of the tour. That translates to the students having free time to settle into their rooms, explore the surrounding area, locate interesting places to eat, or visit the "must see" places not included on the itinerary.

On our 2005 trip to Italy, we arrived in Rome early and were able to check into our rooms by early afternoon, 1:00 p.m. That provided the students with the rest of the afternoon and evening to become acquainted with some of Rome. Both faculty members, Jean Schaefer and I, stationed ourselves in the very small hotel lobby with maps and the list of free-time activities we had suggested for the group (the group received these lists prior to departure, but we have found it doesn't hurt to have extra, just in case) and were prepared to point the groups in the right directions. One group of four wanted to go to the Coliseum; another rather large group was headed for the Castel Sant'Angelo, and still another planned to locate Via del Corso. Armed with their information and directions, the groups headed out for the afternoon and evening. It was not until later that night that Jean and I found out that the group going to the Coliseum became lost on their way back to the hotel. We found out because they are the ones who told us about their adventure. They admitted to being a bit frightened once they realized they were on the wrong bus going in the wrong direction. But there was a certain amount of pride in their voices as they shared how they figured out on their own where they had gone wrong and what they needed to do to correct their mistake and safely return to the hotel. That meant, in their words, "using a lot of hand gestures and pointing to our map to get directions from an Italian who did not speak English." They became the group "experts" at explaining bus schedules to the rest of the group.

Whether it is reading city maps and bus schedules or asking for directions from someone who does not speak the same language, students find they are good at using their problem-solving skills. When the study tours have taken us to Italy, students have found themselves traveling between cities via Eurorail. This is another exciting adventure for many of the students as it is their first experience in train travel. As faculty traveling with the students, we encourage them to read the schedule boards to determine the platform where our train can be found and whether the train is on schedule. For someone who has never tried to decipher a European train schedule board, it becomes an adventure in itself. Once they have mastered this task, however, they become quite confident in their ability, so much so that they have been known to put it to use during free time while in the city of Florence.

During both of our visits to Florence, a number of participants have used unscheduled time to organize their own group trip to Pisa. One or two students take leadership in organizing the trip. They find out the train schedule, cost, and length of time the trip might take, a mere 90 minutes by train from Florence. They also include one or two of the adult members of the group in the excursion. Once at the train station in Pisa, they then have to determine the best way for the group to progress to the Leaning Tower. This means they are finding ways to communicate with Italians when the students do not speak the language. The students always return to the hotel in Florence safe and sound, with wonderful things to say:

> *"It's really unique."*

> *"The setting is not what I expected. I mean the city has grown to the side, not around it [meaning the main cathedral] like everywhere else."*

> *"The postcards do not do it justice."*

It is not unusual, if time allows, that a second group forms for the same excursion with encouragement and advice from the first group. It becomes one of the many times students serve as teachers for the group.

Students have also learned to not take the public-transportation system for granted as well as the importance of paying attention when the bus schedules and routes are being explained to them. During one of the study tours to London, a small group of students decided they would go "clubbing" one night. That is an activity many choose to do during free evening time, and it provides another opportunity to experience the local culture. The more popular clubs are located at some distance from the hotel. This group assumed that the underground, the Tube, ran 24/7 just as it does in most U.S. cities they had visited. Unfortunately for this group of students, that was not the case. The Tube closes down each night at midnight. As this group stayed out a bit past midnight, they missed the last train back to the hotel's neighborhood. They had also not yet taken the time to learn how to read the bus schedule and routes. Therefore this energetic group decided their only alternative was to walk back to the hotel, a distance of more than four miles. That is not a bad walking distance during the day, though at night, or should I say early in the morning, it is a *very* long walk.

After walking for quite some time, the group decided that maybe they should just go ahead and pool their resources and hail a cab. Fortunately one was close at hand. Relieved, they all piled in only to be taken by total surprise when the cab drove a mere two blocks to the hotel. Lesson learned, the next day they figured out how to read the bus schedules and routes.

Whether getting lost in a major world city and finding the way back to the hotel, mastering European train schedules, or just finding their way from one scheduled appointment to the next (and on time), students have self-admittedly become more self-reliant. Students learn quickly how to navigate the public-transportation system and how to read city maps. From one student's post-tour reflection came the following:

> *I became even more self-reliant on this trip. I had to rely on myself to find destinations in a place I didn't know and follow signs I couldn't read. Also, being away from the people I love for this long has been very difficult, but it proved to me that I can do absolutely anything even if I have to do it by myself.*

That is a big step in maturation for many. It is hard to believe that in today's world some college students have never flown anywhere or been to a major city until they go on a study-abroad program. For these students, figuring out a city bus schedule and route is a major accomplishment.

While the students are gaining additional knowledge of and insight into the textile and apparel industry, they are also gaining a greater understanding of a culture different from their own. This becomes very apparent through the simple tasks of finding somewhere to eat or shopping the local markets and shops. The only scheduled meals provided on our tours are breakfasts that come with our hotel stay. In a few instances, we have scheduled a group dinner, but not on every trip.

Students generally take full advantage of the chance to expand their cultural awareness through investigating the various food choices a country has to offer. It is always fun to listen to various small groups compare restaurant or "pub grub" notes in London, trying to decide who found the best food at the best price. Often after these discussions, groups go out to find the restaurant or pub the others were talking about.

These excursions lead to an even greater learning of language and oral communication skills when in Italy. Many Italian restaurants will either have menus with English translations or more commonly an English-speaking waiter. It is fun, though, for all of us to try to order our meal in Italian. We have found the Italian waiters to be quite tolerant of our attempts and helpful with kindly corrections.

On several of our tours, students became quite economical and resourceful by frequenting the grocery and open-air markets. Our students, even though warned ahead of time, are often taken by surprise that they are not allowed to pick up the produce themselves at an open-air Italian food market, or that they are not allowed to purchase only a small amount of a product. Italian markets are where many of the locals shop for their families, so a one-apple purchase is generally not acceptable. Students also discover food products or packaging they have not seen before. Sometimes they can be quite surprised by their purchases. I remember one group purchasing what they thought was a deli-style meal, only to discover once they were back in their hotel room that it was an American equivalent to a microwave meal, and they did not have access to a microwave. Needless to say, they were not overly impressed with their dinner that evening.

Students are encouraged to explore the retail market for textile products, whether a retail chain, a small independent retailer, or an open-air market. Discussions are held prior to departure to acquaint students with the different market and merchandising practices they may encounter. Europeans have long held the reputation of being very trendy and somewhat edgier in their apparel merchandising. Students are required to observe and critique visual merchandise displays in the marketplace. Upon their return to campus, some of the students have incorporated what they have observed into their own displays for the Visual Merchandising and Promotions course.

Although students take advantage of the brick and mortar shops, the markets of Florence really draw their attention. These markets are a study unto themselves, providing the experience for a different kind of retail. Through some of their shopping experiences, students have found that a small-shop owner may also have a stall in one of the markets, selling the same merchandise with a slightly reduced price in the market. The experience also tests their knowledge of textile products studied in the traditional classroom on campus. The students become savvy shoppers, comparing various leather, silk, and wool products. During the first Italy tour in 2001, everyone but the three faculty members returned home with a leather jacket. The 2005 trip to Italy had many of us purchasing silk and cashmere scarves, including the faculty. Did I mention that the students had already checked out the merchandise at one particular stall and deemed it to be of good quality and therefore led the rest of us back there in order for us to make our purchases?

Another cultural retail difference has occurred in both Italy and London during a scheduled visit to fabric stores. One of the highlights in Italy for many U.S. textile and apparel faculty conducting study-abroad short courses similar to mine is a visit to Casa die Tesuti. This generational family-owned fabric store specializes in high-end fabrics. One of the co-owners, Romano Romoli, a gentleman in his mid- to late seventies, gives the most wonderful lecture on the history of the textile industry in Florence, including the development of the various artisan guilds. Romano is a treasure, but what is really unique and somewhat strange for the students relates more to the all-male sales staff. In the United States, it is rare to find an all-male sales staff in a fabric store; occasionally a high-end store similar to Casa dei Tessuti located in the East or major midwestern cities might be staffed with all males. However, it is not a common occurrence. The students are even more amazed when they realize that these gentlemen can determine the exact yardage needed for the student without consulting a pattern envelope that provides the yardage information.

The students who have traveled to London instead of Italy experience something similar during our scheduled visit to Liberty of London. This retailer has a long history, dating back to 1875 when they first opened their doors as the House of Liberty. Many of their fabrics have a distinctive pattern design that creates recognition as a Liberty fabric. The fabric department at Liberty is also staffed by men. The culture shock here is not quite as great as in Casa dei Tessuti, as there are also women working the sales floor in this department. Both the men and women sales staff have the same ability to determine the yardage needed for a particular garment without referring to a sewing pattern.

Harrods has also been a favorite retail experience for the groups visiting London. During our 2003 trip to London, some of us spent a few unscheduled hours in Harrods millinery department trying on hats. Anyone who has seen any of the Royal Family functions on television can imagine the hats available for our enjoyment. Some were totally outrageous, while others were quite normal. The only hat purchased that day was by a student. The hat was not an outrageous royal wedding hat; rather, it was a slouchy straw western-style hat on sale. That particular style was just being introduced here in the United States at that time and has since become quite popular, especially among young women in the Mountain West states. Finding it on sale in Harrods probably meant that the style either did not become a popular one in England, or, more than likely, it was already on its way out of fashion there. Students discover rather quickly that European retailers, unlike those in the United States, only hold sales twice a year, once in January and again in June or July. Our travel time is generally in May, too late for one sale and too early for the other.

When students connect their discipline-based knowledge acquired on campus with what they observe happening in business and industry on the study tours, "ah-ha" moments occur. It is at these times that I know that the experience has been worth it. These moments have occurred on every tour I have coordinated, but I still remember the very first time I observed it happening.

During our 2001 trip to Italy, we toured a silk dyeing and finishing facility near Como. Upon our arrival, we were ushered into a large conference room, where we were shown a brief video of the company and met with the company official conducting the tour. The video and his presentation covered what we would be seeing on the tour as well as some of the history behind fabric printing. As the company guide continued with his presentation, I noticed some of the students making quiet comments to one another. We had covered our expectations of the students' behavior during one of our predeparture meetings, so I was quite disturbed to think the students had forgotten or disregarded the rule concerning giving our guide or company representative our undivided attention. Because I was toward the back of the room, I could not very well give the students "the look" so that they would focus on the company guide and quit their whispering. We soon left the room for the facility tour. During the tour, the students were becoming even more animated in their conversations with one another. Some of the machinery was loud enough that I could not hear what they were saying. Fortunately, that also meant that our guide was no longer speaking and he also could not hear their conversations.

It might have been a good thing if we could have heard them. We both would have been impressed. It was not until the end of the tour, when we were returning to our coach, that I understood what had taken place. At that moment, I also wished that my textile science colleague would have been present to observe this "ah-ha" moment. During the video, the students started to realize that they were going to see in operation the equipment and process that they had studied in their textile science courses. The information covered in the lectures and the photographs in their textbook were about to come to life for them. It was an "ah-ha" moment for me as well when I realized just what this study-tour opportunity was doing for the students.

The students themselves often recognize the value of the study-abroad short-course experience. I would like to share a segment of one student's post-tour reflection from one of the Italian tours, not the same tour as mentioned above:

> I feel that after going on this trip my confidence and self-esteem have risen. After visiting the silk museum and Gucci and Swarovski I feel that I can do anything I put my mind to. I just have to work hard and believe in myself....I feel that I have a fresh start and can go any direction I want. Someday I want to work on a design team, but I want to learn the buying process as well as merchandising. I have considered working with fashion show coordination and also would like to work with the children's theatre in costume construction....I feel inspired by this experience and feel it will aid me in my search for a career. I saw some of the most recent fashions and know this will give me that extra edge that employers keep their eye out for!... I had a blast! Thank you for the wonderful experience.

During one of the London study tours, I received two surprises about knowledge students gained in the classroom. This time, though, the knowledge put into action was from the historic clothing class I teach on campus. Historic Clothing is a course in which students gain insight and knowledge about why and what led to some of the clothing styles of the past. It is also a class during which, as I look out at the students sitting in the classroom, I am faced with looks of boredom and, yes, sometimes even drooping eyelids. I do my best to make it interesting, but for many, history is history no matter what the topic may be.

The first time I was taken by surprise was during our tour of costume and textiles at the Victoria and Albert Museum in London. The textbook used in the historic clothing course has several photo illustrations taken from the "V and A" collection. As we were touring, I was aware that some of the pieces our guide was pointing out were in fact items illustrated in our text. My surprise came when the students started coming up to me and quietly asking if that wasn't in fact the doublet or bodice they had seen pictured in their text. Students were also starting to identify time periods of some of the pieces before the guide had a chance to share the information.

The other proud moment came for me during our tour of the reproduction Globe Theatre. We had tickets for the evening's performance with a tour of the theater scheduled beforehand. With the tour complete, we had time for a quick meal and a self-guided tour of the small museum area before the evening's performance. The group broke into smaller groups to tour the museum. As with most museums, some individuals lingered a bit longer over some of the exhibits than others. In the lower level of the museum, the Globe had created a Renaissance setting complete with house interior vignettes. One area was textile related. I came upon a group of our students with a couple of our nonstudent participants. The nonstudents were asking the students about the exhibit and what the different items were. The students handled the questions like experts, explaining the various items displayed as if they did this sort of thing every day. They repeated the concepts and information from my lectures and the course readings. I guess it really did sink in somewhat.

Sometimes the students' "ah-ha" moments become "uh-oh" moments for me. On this same London trip, students shared with me and some of the other adults on the tour their experience from an evening out. Several of the students had decided to go out one evening and take in the London night life. As a faculty member, I always wonder just what knowledge students take away from my classes, especially the course on social psychology of dress that I teach. I often wonder if I impart in them a thirst for higher knowledge and ideals. Do I create in them an understanding of the theoretical framework of the research we are studying? Have they fully grasped the concepts in the social psychology of dress? The answer, unfortunately, is "no." I found, much to my chagrin, that the one thing they remembered from my Clothing in Modern Society course was the differences between a transvestite and a drag queen. Evidently during their evening out, they observed someone that part of the group felt sure was a drag queen, while the rest of the group believed they were observing a transvestite. They were still debating the differences and which category this individual fell into the next morning when they shared the story with the rest of us. So much for my attempts to teach the social psychology of clothing theory.

So What Do I Have to Do for Credit?

Student assessment can be both formal and informal in a study-tour setting. All of our study tours to date have incorporated both. The study tour in the Department of Family and Consumer Sciences actually starts weeks before the departure date. Once the individual participants have made an initial monetary deposit, the group is set and the predeparture meetings start.

As many as six meetings throughout the semester occur prior to tour departure. Each meeting can last from one to two hours, and we have even held an all-day Saturday session for the interdisciplinary tours. Attendance at these meetings and all scheduled tour appointments are mandatory for those enrolling for study-tour credit. Others, not receiving credit, are highly encouraged to attend. As previously mentioned, these meetings are held to communicate with the group and share important details of the planned tour.

In addition to trip itineraries, safety and health issues, processing of necessary forms, and understanding the rules of the tour, these meeting times serve as an opportunity for group members to become better acquainted with one another and the country or countries they will visit. Activities and discussions held during these scheduled meetings are designed for this purpose.

It is not uncommon to have repeat travelers on our study tours. They are encouraged to share something from their past experiences with those who have not gone before. Of course the faculty share information about cultural and historic sites and industries on the itinerary. Faculty have also been known to prepare an Italian meal for the group during the all-day session for the last Italy tour.

In addition, we explore cultural differences between the United States and the country or countries to be visited. In the case of the Italy tours, participants are handed a simple language guide, and a small amount of time is spent reviewing the guide and encouraging students to try the words and phrases listed. Before the 2005 Italy tour, Italian phrases could be heard in the hallway outside of the textile and merchandising classrooms. In their post-tour evaluations, many students say that they wished they would have learned more Italian phrases before they left for Italy. Go figure.

Faculty also use the time during these meetings to discuss course requirements. A daily journal is required for all of the students enrolled in the FCSC study-tour course. Rather than allowing students to develop their own or use a notebook for this journal, I have created one that they use. There is a dated journal page for each day of travel. On this page students record their activities for the day, including scheduled visits as well as free-time activities. They are then asked to respond to the following three questions: (a) Overall, how did you feel about the day's experiences? (b) Did you gain any new ideas that will help you in either personal or professional growth? and (c) Any further comments about the day's activities?

I have found through conversations with other faculty coordinators of study-abroad courses that they also use a required daily journal. It provides a way to monitor whether the students are taking advantage of all the program has to offer. During the scheduled premeetings we, the faculty, share options the students may want to consider for the free time in their tour schedule. These suggestions can include anything from additional museums, to special shopping districts, to additional cultural attractions.

During the 2005 Italy tour, two art majors spent a day attempting to visit almost every gallery or Roman art history piece they had ever studied. Their daylong adventure took them throughout the city for a day they will never forget. They located the sights on the city map and determined their best route and mode of transportation. We, the faculty, were amazed at their determination and chutzpah in pulling off such a feat. They were exhausted by day's end but had an air of confidence that only comes from achieving a long-held difficult goal. They were as excited by their success as any world-class athlete upon winning a gold medal. Their learning about themselves and the art history pieces they saw far exceeded what most of us can achieve in a traditional on-campus semester-long course. It took independent thought and critical thinking on both their parts for the day to be a success. Without the benefit of the daily journal, we, the faculty, might not have recognized the full impact of their daylong adventure. Through the journal exercise, both students described themselves as introverts. Incidentally, one of the students shared in her journal entry that she had never done anything without her best friend before, and that day's activity had "helped me overcome some of my shyness. I now feel more confident to do more things on my own."

By recording their activities in the journal, students may also be more willing to experience new things while traveling. Who really wants to admit in writing that they spent their free time in their hotel room? However, some end up doing just that. Or they might fill all of their free time looking for the next McDonald's for lunch, or they might spend all of their time and money in a giant European shopping spree without noticing the differences in merchandising techniques or even the products offered for sale compared to what is found in the States. It is unfortunate that this still happens, but through the journal, the faculty has more information than just observations of student behavior on which to base their assessment. The journal is a good way to hold the students accountable.

The journal is not the only written requirement for our study tours. Students are also required to research some aspect of the textile and fashion industry of the tour country. They are encouraged to include information on at least one of the industries or designers they are scheduled to visit. I have required this paper to be completed before the departure date, and I have also set the due date for one month after our return. If I set the due date for after our return, I do require evidence of the references or a rough draft to be submitted prior to departure. This forces the students into prestudy of the country and industry they will visit. With a due date after our return, the students are able to include personal observations and reflections in their papers. I also require that the students write a one- to two-page tour reflection paper on the flight home to be handed to me upon our arrival at our home airport. I spend the return flight reading and critiquing their journals while they share their more memorable moments on paper for me to read later. I also encourage students to use this reflection as a critique of the study tour. It is the students' opportunity to share with me what has worked and what has not.

Student behavior is also assessed based on "rules of travel" developed for our study tours. Some of the rules address safety concerns, and others address a code of conduct that we expect students to follow. The following list contains some of the "rules" we have developed for study tours:

- Travel in groups during free-time activities, at a very minimum of two.
- Be on time for scheduled appointments.
- Keep credit and debit cards in a secure place; using a hidden neck or belt wallet or the in-room safe found in many hotels is recommended.
- Carry only the amount of cash you anticipate needing for one day; the amount will vary based on country and the current value of the U.S. dollar.
- Contact one of the faculty members immediately if there is a safety issue or health concern.
- Act responsibly and dress appropriately; appropriate dress includes clothing of a more modest nature than students may be used to wearing on campus as well as appearing neat and clean at all times.
- Learn the local currency.
- Learn basic language phrases and words for countries visited.

These rules and expectations for student behavior and participation are covered during the predeparture meetings. It is made clear, both orally and in writing, that violations of the expectations and rules will result in disciplinary action. If a participant's behavior becomes the cause for embarrassment for the group or the University of Wyoming as a whole, the participant will be removed from the group and will be responsible for his or her own return to the United States, including cost. Cultural differences in acceptable behavior are discussed during these predeparture meetings. We try to ensure no surprises as to the expectations of the participants. Above all, we want to ensure that the University of Wyoming is not given as an example of unacceptable behavior in articles focusing on study-abroad programs. In the recent past, there have been several instances of this among other institutions.

Can My Mom Go Too?

With the first university study tour I conducted, New York City in the early 1980s, I was asked if someone's relative could go with us. Although the focus of these programs is educational, I have always been willing to open the study tours to others. "Others" have included mothers, sisters, alumni, other university faculty, and staff. There are advantages and disadvantages to this arrangement, but I believe the advantages outweigh the disadvantages.

Initially I felt that by opening the opportunity of our study tours to others I would secure enough travel participants to make the planning and expense worthwhile for all involved. Many of the travel agencies or tour companies providing study-tour programs offer a rate reduction if the number of participants reaches a certain level. Because of my enthusiasm for international travel, I like to see as many students participate as possible. Often the opportunity to travel translates to the per-student cost. If I can keep the cost "reasonable," then maybe more students would be able to travel. Not a bad plan if it works, and up to a point it has. The biggest disadvantage I see of opening the study tour to those other than university students occurs when the size of the group becomes too large. This was almost the case in 2005 when we took thirty-three individuals to Italy. Even with two faculty members to share the responsibility, the group size was almost too large.

Having parents, other university faculty and staff, and alumni on the study tours has created a bonus I had not initially anticipated. As a student of adult education, I embrace the concept of lifelong learning. As a faculty member, it is a concept I hope my students come to understand and embrace as well. What I did not realize was that by allowing older adults to participate in our study tours, I was creating a setting for the undergraduates to observe lifelong learning in action.

Older adult students generally have no problem asking questions in an educational setting, including when that setting is in a factory, a designer showroom, a museum, or a retail store in a foreign city. The traditional undergraduate, on the other hand, can have trouble asking a question in a "regular" classroom. The older participants' willingness to ask questions at scheduled appointments opens the door for information exchange to take place. I also have observed that, rather than being embarrassed by the questions, traditional students become more aware of what is being said, and, in many cases, their interest level increases. The business or industry individuals with whom we meet also seem to take a greater interest in our group.

During the 2003 London tour, we were scheduled to tour a textile mill in Galashiels, Scotland. This mill manufactures wool tartans as well as cashmere. The entire weaving and finishing processes of tartans take place at the mill in Galashiels. The tour was to be an hour long, with time for a visit to the retail shop at the end of the tour. We were halfway through the tour of the facility when I realized that we only had fifteen minutes left for the scheduled tour. The scheduled hour-long tour took our group an hour and a half. The reason for the additional length was the interest our group demonstrated in the processes they were shown. This interest was made apparent when the questions started with the older nonstudent participants. The questions raised by the nonstudents encouraged the students to ask their own questions. The textile mill was pleased with our group and in fact called our agent in London the next morning and asked to please send more groups like ours!

On this same tour, we had a scheduled appointment to visit the workroom of fashion designer Zandra Rhodes, to meet with her head designer. Again, the nonstudents started asking the questions. This seemed to break the ice for the younger people in the group, and they too started asking questions. Some of these questions led to a friendly debate between Ben (no last name needed; we just know him as Ben), the head designer, and me over which method of pattern development was best. Ben almost exclusively utilizes draping for his design work, whereas I prefer using the flat pattern method. The students and adults both found this friendly debate fun and enlightening. They were able to hear the advantages as well as disadvantages of each method from both "experts." Ben and I were both careful to make sure we explained that, though most styles can be created with either method, some styles are better created using one method rather the other. Draping works best for soft, flowing styles, and flat pattern works best for more tailored, fitted styles. Zandra Rhodes's designs are mainly soft, flowing styles. Ben encouraged, in fact insisted, that members of the group model for one another the sample garments found in the workroom. It was fun to observe the interaction and encouragement given to one another during this informal modeling session. Older and younger were trying on clothes, laughing, and taking pictures of one another. It was a great intergenerational bonding experience. It is a rare opportunity to visit a designer's workroom, let alone be allowed to try on the model garments. Many of the students recognized at trip's end that it is not something they would have been able to do if they were not part of a study-tour group such as ours. One student commented, "I wanted the chance to go to designers' places and see what they really do. Thank you for that opportunity."

My Reflections

I would not trade the experiences I have had traveling with students for anything. My life and my teaching are richer because of these experiences. I have more examples of new trends in merchandising and design to share with students in the classroom when I return from a study tour. Along with the students, I have a list of industry contacts made through these study tours. As I finish this writing, I am preparing to leave in a few months' time for another study-abroad experience—this time for London, and I am adding Paris to the itinerary. I recently asked this new group to write down their reasons for wanting to go on this tour as well as what they expect to get out of the experience. One student stated it quite simply when she wrote, "I am going on the trip because I want to see the world. I think that people who travel and experience different ways of life are much more open-minded than others. I also just love to travel!"

The most important reason for me is the privilege of getting to know the students on a different level than normally possible and introducing them to cultures other than their own. I have been present during an "ah-ha" moment, when it suddenly dawns on them that the manufacturing process they are observing is the same one that Dr. Cameron lectured about in their textile science class, or when they meet a head designer in his workroom and realize he uses the same techniques that Dr. Brown and I have been teaching them. I am thrilled when I see the excitement in their eyes as they stand in Piazza San Marco in Venice for the first time or they see in real life a fifteenth-century textile in a museum referenced in their textbook. A student summed up her "ah-ha" moments with the following statement in her evaluation: "I am proud of myself, being able to go places without the whole group and successfully use maps and mass transit. Also, I found myself enjoying the 'moment' of my tour experience and getting lost in the Italian zest for life." Seldom do moments like those occur in the traditional classroom. For those of us involved with study-tour programs, the world truly is our classroom.

Postscript

In Great Britain, *loo* is slang for *restroom*. To ask for directions in Italian, it is best to have a map and itinerary handy and learn to say, "*Dove* (doe vay)…?"

7

Rachel Watson

R achel Watson is from Leadville, Colorado, a tiny mining community at 10,152 feet. She earned her undergraduate degree in chemistry from the University of Denver in 1998 and a master of science from the University of Wyoming (UW) in 2001. She is a lifelong student, currently enrolled in the E.D.D. program in instructional technology at UW, where she has been teaching for six years. Her courses include General Chemistry, Principles of Biochemistry, General Microbiology, General and Medical Microbiology Labs, and Clinical Biochemistry Lab. She is also a passionate cross-country skier and has been the co-coach of the university's club team for almost nine years.

Listen for the Dune Buggies

Learner-Centered Teaching

Another semester has come to an end. I stand alone in the microbiology teaching lab, with only one bank of lights turned on. I remove the old student posters from the walls and replace them with this year's new efforts. In a room that is characterized day in and day out with lively students, the silence seems strange, sad. I pin up the last poster, pile my arms full of miscellaneous items that need to be returned to my office, and open the door to leave the room. As I do, I turn around and slowly dim the lights. Tiny tears collect in the corners of my eyes as I reflect on the semester. As the light clicks off, the room goes dark and I only hope that next semester's students will be half as amazing, as special, as those that I had this semester.

Thoughts of students flood my mind as I walk back to my office. With blurry vision, I fit the key into the lock and precariously deposit the items from the lab. I find my way to my desk chair and simply sit for a moment. It is hard to believe that it has been more than six years since I stepped into the classroom for the first time. I can remember how nervous I was. I was in graduate school, every day becoming more and more intimate with my lab pipetmen, when somehow I had been convinced to teach a summer chemistry class for the Upward Bound and Math Science Initiative High School Program. The room they had scheduled for me was in the Physical Sciences Building. I arrived on the first day of class, wrote the introductory material on the board and checked to see that the technology was functional. I sat in different student seats to be sure that everyone could see, closed shades here, opened shades there, until the lighting was just right. I glanced down at my watch, just two and a half hours until class. I had spent the rest of the time shared between checking my appearance in the bathroom mirrors and nervously trying to study my notes.

Funny, in six years so much has changed, and then again, so little. No matter how many times I teach a class, no matter how many days a week I see the students, I am still nervous each time I step into the classroom.

I glance around my office. My eyes flicker over pictures of students on the wall, and my mind quickly returns to that first summer, to a faculty meeting where I sat listening to the other teachers talk about their struggle with the Upward Bound students. They commiserated about everything from the students' disrespect to their inability to learn. Although I tried to be patient, it was a precious few minutes before I could handle no more. I stood up and said that if they treated their students with respect, their students would pay them the same favor. I had left that meeting with so many emotions, but I realized what I had said was truly what guided my teaching. Later that night, after the passion of the day had begun to wane, I sat down and wrote what, with multiple revisions and time, became the following saying: "*Treat the person sitting next to you as if he or she has accomplished amazing things; you will never be wrong, and you will certainly never be sorry.*" Now, as the tears begin to clear from my eyes, I stare at this saying where it hangs, clumsily taped to my office wall. Since the day that I wrote it, or perhaps even before I put it into words, this saying has guided my pedagogy. If I treat students as though they have knowledge valuable to the class, to our learning as a group, they will treat me in the same way. I have never met a student who didn't teach me something, who didn't have a contribution to make.

I marvel as I realize that in the years that have passed, I have been so lucky to get to know almost two thousand students. Sometimes I think I will not be able to make it through any more semesters. When each class comes to an end and each group of students leaves, it is as though a piece of my heart goes too. I never know how I will be able to muster enough energy to start the whole semester-long journey again. But then I think about how much fun it is to watch new students learn and to follow students through the years as they pass from one class to the next.

I think about James. We met for the first time when he was a student in the Math Science Initiative Project and a senior in high school. The next year, as a freshman in college, James was a student again in the Chemistry 1020 course that I taught. Just two years later I welcomed James back to the classroom once more when he enrolled in General Microbiology. I smile as I think that even right now, as I write, James is probably packing for his next adventure as a graduate student in chemistry. These thoughts of James bring to mind his friend Josh. I will never forget the day that, as a freshman, Josh bounced into my office to make suggestions that would forever change the way in which I wrote exams. I often miss Josh, as he became an inextricable part of General Microbiology. He took the class three years ago and then assisted with teaching until he graduated and went on to pursue a fellowship with the National Institutes of Health. I wonder how he is doing now as he prepares for his next adventure in medical school. Thoughts of one student only lead to another: Chris and Amy in medical school, Liz finishing graduate school, Katie in Poland, Greg trying to decide between a career in medicine or the priestly ministry, and Chase studying birds at the Teton Science School.

A list of reflections of my students could consume an entire book, but perhaps none of these memories stand out more than those of Micah. A quick smile and laugh pass across my face as I recall a character who was quite possibly the biggest bundle of energy to ever set foot in the microbiology classroom. Never did Micah miss an opportunity to contribute commentary, poke fun, or otherwise add character to a day's lecture. I've often wished that I could permanently seed Micah in every classroom just to stimulate student interaction. After his semester as a student, Micah honored us by committing to be a teaching assistant. I loved to watch Micah lecture and interact with students. His unbridled enthusiasm and compassion made him a phenomenal teacher. However, I remember one day in particular when Micah surprised me. True to character, he had opened the lecture with a joke; this had captivated the students' undivided attention. However, after the joke, Micah began to discipline the students, reprimanding them for the poor quality of their lab reports. He then turned his back to the students and launched into an excruciatingly long account of the way in which he writes lab reports, the "correct" way. As it is my policy to never question my teaching assistants in front of the students, I simply breathed a sigh and removed my bright-pink pen from the lapel pocket of my bright-pink lab coat and wrote a second saying that is now taped, next to the first, on my office wall: *"The goal of teaching is not to show students how much we know, but instead to help students realize their own capacity to know."*

I stare at the sayings on the wall and realize that together they define my learner-centered teaching philosophy. Although different, both really express the importance of listening. One can never help students realize their capacity to know unless we listen to what they already know and have learned. In order to treat a person as though she or he has accomplished amazing things, one has to listen to what that student has to say and acknowledge its value. I shake my head as I realize that many traditional teaching methods could not be further from achieving these goals. In the two stories that I tell in this chapter, I reflect upon ways in which I have carried the sayings on the wall into the classroom, the ways that I have tried to truly listen to students.

I'd Rather Be a Dune Buggy

It is the first day of the fall semester and, as is true only on this day, students have arrived twenty minutes early and are all crowded into the foyer outside of the auditorium. With butterflies of nerves and excitement in my stomach, I slowly wheel my teaching cart into the foyer and look around. Several dozen nervous pairs of eyes flicker in my direction, questioning, curious. The atmosphere is tense. A few students smile, and I take a moment to introduce myself. In turn they tell me their names, and I make a conscious effort to memorize as many of them as possible. I return to my teaching cart to make sure I have remembered everything. I inventory several demos, three textbooks, overhead sheets, Sharpies, stuffed microorganisms, note cards, lab manuals, my computer, and a projector. I close my eyes. My mind flickers to my class from the previous semester and how much I already miss them. I turn my mind to the class period to come. Sadness creeps into my mind as I remember that, this summer, a committee of which I was not a member rewrote my syllabus. The rewritten syllabus asks me to cover more material in less time and affords no flexibility. I tell myself that this time I will not question this schedule and that I will simply and quickly present it as it is. I will not take time to express my concerns or listen to student concerns. I will not tell them I believe such a schedule does not put student learning as the primary priority. I will conform. And, most importantly, I will certainly not repeat my actions of this summer when, on the first day of class, on the spur of the moment, I said to the students, "This is what I think of the tentative schedule!" and ripped it into pieces.

I open my eyes to a flurry of motion and realize that students from the class prior to ours have begun to leave. I take a deep breath and push my cart down the aisle and to the front of the large auditorium. As I bumble and proceed to drop things, an eager student who had previously introduced himself as Jeff, a predental major, kindly picks up things that I have left in my wake. The professor from the previous class informs me that the projector is not working, and I smile, knowing I bought my own for just these moments. The students nervously settle into their chairs. I try to make them feel more comfortable by smiling, but the anticipation is still high and students are still fearful. I distribute syllabi and begin by introducing myself.

"Please," I say, "you will show me the most respect if you simply call me Rachel. If you call my phone looking for Ms. Watson, I will think you are a salesman and quickly hang up. If you call me Dr. Watson, I will look around for Sherlock Holmes." A few students chuckle and seem to relax a bit. I continue and try to impress upon the students the breadth and importance of microbiology. My own nerves begin to subside slightly, and I feel them exude a familiar and welcome enthusiasm. I walk through the room and talk about the role microorganisms play in bioremediation and genetic engineering. I inform them that without microorganisms, every food chain on Earth would become extinct. My eyes scan the room. Some of the students seem alert, attentive, and excited. Still others are unsure, cautious. I identify a young man sitting in the back of the room. I approach him and ask him his name.

"Aaron," I say, "you don't look like you're understanding the true importance of microorganisms. Let me try to better impress upon you the gravity of the situation. Aaron, without microbes there would be no more beer, no more beer!" Aaron smiles, and his response is drowned by almost thunderous laughter. This roar of laughter fuels my own enthusiasm, and I begin to feel the personality of this new group of students.

But I am quickly pulled away from the sheer enjoyment of the moment as I realize that, if I am to stay on schedule, I must finish reviewing the syllabus and cover a great deal of material by the end of the period. I tune out the students and am able to stay on track for quite some time. I quickly motor through most components of the syllabus and, for a few long minutes, I take no time for questions or interaction. I tell myself that I must hurry; I must cover more material; I must not take time for explanation, or questions, or thought. I must go faster. But, as I turn to the last page of the syllabus, I look up and I feel a horrible pang. My stomach feels hollow. And for what seems like an eternity, I stare into the wondering eyes of the students and I hear a cry from inside, saying, *No, they deserve better! The goal of teaching is not to show students how much we know, but instead to help students realize their own capacity to know.* I look down at the schedule, my head swims, and, just as I had this summer, I know what has to be done. I look right into the eyes of my students and say slowly with every ounce of sincerity, "I hate this, I just hate this schedule!"

Then with growing confidence, a filling of the hollow in my stomach, and a piercing sense that I am doing the right thing, I say, "This schedule is like a railroad track; there is no option for deviation from the path. We are like a train along this track, and I am the conductor. If I follow the track, I am forced to proceed at maximum speed. You, as students, are the passengers with no control over either the route or the speed. As I speed down the track, you are all flying out of the window, screaming, 'Rachel, please slow down!'" The students laugh, and I can tell they are visualizing the insanity of the scenario. I can tell too that, sadly, it is a very familiar scene.

I look again at the syllabus and then put it down. I say, "I would rather that we be dune buggies, riding over the sand, exploring every facet of the desert but doing it in any way or direction that we choose." I'm quiet for a moment. And then, as I have for every semester since I began teaching, I feel the students' approval. I can tell they appreciate my honesty and the fact that I trust them to help guide their own learning.

"So," I say, "this semester we will try to introduce most of the facets of microbiology, to visit many of the stops along the railroad track, but we will accomplish this goal on dune buggies. We will never be too busy to stop for questions, discussions, or to explore applications. We will never go on until we are comfortable with the current material."

As I make this statement, I am fueled only by the optimism that I feel and the excitement and appreciation that I sense from my students. It will be several more months before I will read an article in the *Denver Post* describing the work of Nobel laureate Carl Wieman. After winning the Nobel Prize in 2001, Wieman turned his attention to teaching innovation in undergraduate physics courses. I will read this article on Sunday, the 19th day of March, and be moved to tears as I read that one of Wieman's central goals of reform is spending more time covering fewer topics in class, never moving on until he is certain that students understand. It will be even longer before I read a 1997 article by David Hammer in which he approaches, head on, the tension that educators feel between promoting student inquiry and covering course content. In this article, published in *Cognition and Instruction,* he will introduce to me, for the first time, *discovery learning,* which he defines as "a form of curriculum in which students are exposed to particular questions and experiences in such a way that they 'discover' for themselves the intended concepts." He explains that, although educators view inquiry-based objectives as being extremely important, they are usually sacrificed for the certainty of traditional content-based objectives as they are easier to assess. But, as I smile at the students in the large lecture hall on this first day of class, I know nothing about either Carl Wieman or David Hammer. I only know that it feels really good to hand the students the keys to their own dune buggies.

Grading with New Ears

Knowing a speaker will deepen one's understanding of her speech.

(Marjorie L. DeVault, *Liberating Method*)

After gathering together pencils in every color of the rainbow and spending about half an hour sufficiently sharpening each one, I root through my desk drawer for my "You Rock My World" stickers. I simply can't start grading exams until I am armed with what one might consider "comfort paraphernalia." I pause for a moment and reflect on another busy semester. One would think that after ten such semesters and the grading of what now totals somewhere upwards of fifty thousand exams, I could simply sit down to grade without anxiety. However, nothing could be further from the truth. While I love every facet of teaching, it is grading that I find the most difficult.

I finally sit down and begin to unload the Rubbermaid bin that is stuffed to the gills with exams. I pile them into a stack on my office table and organize the key. It was the final exam of the semester and was a difficult, application-based take-home. I momentarily grumble to myself, Why couldn't I simply use a pure multiple-choice format? The question is rhetorical, as I know that I only truly recognize student learning, or lack thereof, when I take time to read through their work. Finally the readying process is complete, and I begin with the first free-response question. One by one, I roll back the front pages of the exam, and one by one I grade the same question on each student's paper. I pay special attention to consistency and objectivity. A good answer should be a good answer, regardless of the writer. As the grader, I should simply view the answer and translate it to the points that it is worth. The "correct," or "true," answer should transcend any ties that it has to the writer. But as I shuffle each exam from the "to do" pile, past my eyes for assessment, and into the "done" stack, I feel the increasing need to peer at the identity of the writer.

For a moment I stop and truly ponder the existence of objectivity. One of the core ambitions of science is certainly the attempt to achieve it. We strive to be able to interpret our data in an unbiased way, to assess sources without preconceived notions, and to have our desires for project outcomes affect our actual interpretations of the results as little as possible. To reflect this professional detachment from our data, we write all of our professional articles in third person. In teaching science courses, at any level, it is common to ask students to write their lab reports and research papers in strictly third person, to try to erase any tracks that they, as researchers or writers, may have left behind. Perhaps these attempts work, perhaps we come closer to revealing the true nature of our world when we make them? My mind is drawn to Alan D. Sokal and what has now been popularized and wildly debated as the Sokal affair. In a 1996 issue of *Social Text*, he published an article that he later states in the online *Lingua Franca* was "liberally salted with nonsense." He goes on to state, "I intentionally wrote the article so that any competent physicist or mathematician (or undergraduate physics or math major) would realize that it is a spoof." Sokal attributes the acceptance of this falsified article to the fact that the editors of *Social Text* liked the article's conclusion as well as to the fact that it sounded good and flattered the editors. Sokal then launches into an emotional diatribe attacking the postmodern leftists and their willingness to blur the boundaries between the truth of science and our interpretations of it. It seems almost stunning that Sokal never considers that he may have been granted publication simply based upon the fact that he is a well-known, highly respected physics researcher. In the ten years prior to publishing this falsified article in *Social Text,* the Thomson Corporation's Web of Science shows that he had published more than thirty articles in respected physics journals. Might this show that once an author is well known, we have difficulty reading the work in search of quality divorced from the name? Perhaps this acknowledgment would only have proven the postmodern point, further blurring the line between the truth (or in this case falsehood) of science and the identity of the researcher. Certainly Alan Sokal would not have wanted this, as it is against this very point that he is so ardently fighting.

My mind hurtles back to a recent course I took called Applied Feminist Theories and Methods. It was in this course that I was introduced, for the first time, to the feminist critique of science. Scholars such as Sandra Harding question the idea that a researcher can ever achieve true objectivity, or value neutrality, in which scientific truths can somehow escape any ties to historical context, values, situation, or agendas of the researcher. They query whether a researcher can truly be simply a vessel through which the truth of science makes itself known. Marjorie DeVault explains in her book *Liberating Method: Feminism and Social Research,* "Such emerging feminist formulations repudiate the traditional version of objectivity that requires a separation of knower and known." In fact, many feminist methodologists prescribe to methods that value subjectivity or at least do not deny the inevitability of its existence. In doing so, these methods acknowledge social situation and historical context. It could be argued that in recognizing the inevitability of subjectivity, a better type of "objectivity" is actually obtained, one in which not only what is being said is questioned but also who has said it and the context in which it was said. Harding refers to this new type of objectivity as "strong objectivity."

I look up from the exam that has now become a blur and wonder if acknowledgment of the inevitability of subjectivity in grading has ever really been explored. Would "strong objectivity" actually enhance the intellectual rigor of my grading process? I look back down at the exam in front of me. The question that I am currently grading presents a hypothetical situation in which one of the students in the class has "walking pneumonia." Students are asked to suggest an antibiotic to treat the disease and explain their choice. I read the student's answer. It is scientifically stated and technically correct; the method proposed would effectively treat the patient. However, I can find no similarity between the therapy proposed by the student and the methods I expected students to propose based on our classroom discussions and the textbook. I am about to write a nasty comment on the paper, accusing the student of plagiarism and reminding the student that it is essential to cite every outside source, when I can handle it no longer, flip to the front cover, and peer at the name. It takes no more than one glance for me to realize that the identity of the writer is truly important to understanding what she has written. Shelly is a certified nursing assistant (CNA). Every day she comes to class dressed in scrubs after a long night at work. I reread her exam answer and realize that she has likely had many work-related experiences that allow her to answer the question in a nonstandard way. My usual exam doldrums are replaced, at least momentarily, by a sense of newfound student advocacy. I finish with Shelly's exam and flip to the next student. It is Kelly. I read through the response and make more sense of it as I remember that Kelly often confuses the words *contemplate* and *compensate*. She did it just the other day during office hours. Next is Lynlee. She struggles to express herself in writing; finding words for her knowledge is difficult, but I remember from the review sessions that she usually gets it right after a few tries. I read through her answer, which seems largely incorrect, but there, in the corner, the last thing she wrote, that's exactly right! Next is Chris's exam; he is a great student, and his response should be a joy to read. I flip to the correct page and notice the question was never completed. Something must be wrong. I patter over to the computer and shoot out an e-mail: "Chris, I noticed that you struggled a bit on the exam. Is everything okay? Is there anything that I can do to help?"

I am elated; I realize that knowing whose work it is allows me to recognize and understand nontraditional vocabulary. Being familiar with how a student talks allows me to better understand his or her exam response. Identifying the writer of the response allows me to recognize the unexpected struggle of a good student and, likewise, unexpected improvement in a student who has struggled.

I've finally finished grading the first exam question. I ready myself to tackle the next question, which asks students to compare the amount of energy generated when *Bacillus subtilis* (an aerobic bacterium) fully oxidizes

1.3×10^{12} molecules of glucose versus the same number of molecules of the fat palmitate. I pull the next exam off the stack. It is Ryan's. He works so hard, attends lecture every day, and comes to office hours and every review. Most recently he has been struggling with metabolism, especially glycolysis and the first committed step catalyzed by phosphofructokinase (PFK). He can simply never remember the name of the enzyme, where it goes, and what it does. We must have spent over an hour drawing and reviewing all the pathways on the board last Friday. I read his response and am ecstatic! Everything looks perfect. *You Rock My World, Ryan,* I think to myself as I move on to the next exam. It is Aaron's. Aaron is an incredibly intelligent, dedicated young man. In fact, he is the top student in the class. I wonder how his knee is doing? He had injured it earlier in the semester and had worried that it might be a torn ligament. This has caused him much strife as he loves to alpine ski, and he and his girlfriend had, for the first time, purchased season tickets to Winter Park ski area in Colorado.

I try to bring my mind back from this momentary tangent but realize it was not without value. My grading can only be enhanced by "strong objectivity" because I truly know my students!

I remember back to a teaching colloquium I had attended in the spring of 2002. A particular day, no, a particular *comment* nags at my memory. We were sitting as a group speaking about students who fail, students who just never live up to expectations. The comments were varied, but most explained these students by saying they just do not apply themselves, do not understand what it takes to succeed. However, after a few moments of charged debate, a counseling professor looked up, and in an alarmingly calm voice, he said, "I think we just haven't found the right way to listen." I pondered this statement for so many days, years in fact, and for the first time now I feel that I truly "get it." By acknowledging the social situation of each one of my students, I had found a new way to listen.

Treat the person sitting next to you as if he or she has accomplished amazing things; you will never be wrong, and you will certainly never be sorry. My grading realizations bring me a step closer to this goal taped on my wall, as I will only be able to achieve it by recognizing that "amazing accomplishments" are unique to the individual. If we predefine with a syllabus or grading key what amazing is, we also preselect a limited membership! I find myself very much in agreement with Marjorie DeVault when she says, "The critical point is that feminist researchers can be conscious of listening as process, and can work on learning to listen in ways that are personal, disciplined, and sensitive to difference."

Suggested Reading

Brown, Jennifer. 2006. "Canadian lure reels in CU Nobelist Wieman." *Denver Post*, March 19, 8A.

DeVault, Marjorie L. 1999. *Liberating Method: Feminism and Social Research.* Philadelphia: Temple University Press.

Gelsthorpe, Loraine. 1992. Response to Martyn Hammersley's paper "On feminist methodology." *Sociology* 26(2):213–18.

Hammer, David. 1997. Discovery learning and discovery teaching. *Cognition and Instruction* 15(4):485–529.

Harding, Sandra. 2004. "Rethinking Standpoint Epistemology, What is 'Strong Objectivity?'" In *Feminist Perspectives on Social Research*, edited by S.N. Hesse-Biber and M.L. Yaiser. New York: Oxford University Press.

Sokal, Alan D. 1996. A physicist experiments with cultural studies. *Lingua Franca* May 1996: 62–64.

———. 1996. Transgressing the boundaries: Toward a transformative hermeneutics of quantum gravity. *Social Text* 46/47:217–52.

The Thomson Corporation. 2006. Web of Science. Available through the University of Wyoming Library Web site, www-lib.uwyo.edu/find/articles.cfm (accessed August 9, 2006).

8

Raina M. Spence

Raina Spence began working with the University of Wyoming in the summer of 2002. She graduated that same year with an M.S. in plant pathology from Washington State University. Currently Spence serves as the Master Gardener state coordinator for Wyoming. When not traveling throughout the state training master gardeners, Spence is an avid hiker and artist. She parlays her vocation into an avocation, utilizing many horticultural themes in her works of art. Traveling is another passion, which takes her all over the globe. She enjoys incorporating her travel experiences into her lectures and shares information about international agriculture with the citizens of Wyoming.

Gardening, Growing, and Gathering Across Generations

Of course, there is no absolute assurance that those things I plant will always fall upon arable land and will take root and grow, nor can I know if another cultivator did not leave contrary seeds before I arrived. I do know, however, that if I leave little to chance, if I am careful about the kinds of seeds I plant, about their potency and nature, I can, within reason, trust my expectations.

(from Maya Angelou's "At Harvesttime,"
in *Wouldn't Take Nothing for My Journey Now*)

Many such inspirational quotes exist in popular literature. Quotes to instill confidence and courage are rattled off to young undergraduates by professors preparing to launch their pupils out into the world. All such deep and lofty thoughts are banished from the mind when you stand before an audience consisting of individuals old enough to be your grandparents with the charge of teaching them something about gardening, an avocation that most have been engaged in longer than you have been alive. Such is my story. Finding the courage to embrace positive expectations and will them into reality within the realms of my teaching duties did not occur without a fair number of trials.

Twenty-three. When represented in years, it seemed like a formidable number. Slightly over two decades to read voraciously, study obsessively, and tuck knowledge tightly into the crevices of the young brain. It's just enough time to obtain a master's degree, land a first "professional job," and move out to Wyoming to start down the path of a promising career. A century ago, it would have been considered middle-aged. But in the twenty-first century, 23 years of age certainly smacks of youth. Upon arrival at the College of Agriculture, I had to admit this to myself. My bell-bottom jeans, butterfly hairclips, and ability to recite the words to nearly every alternative rock song on the radio certainly set me apart from my colleagues. Anyone could have picked me out of a lineup. I was the one without the cowboy boots, Copenhagen-bulged smile, and knowledge of the local ranching culture. I lacked the luxury of being able to relate to the public based solely upon decades of experience, gray hairs, or an impressive doctoral degree. If I was to be a success in this environment, I would have to find a niche. More precisely, I would have to create a niche.

Born and raised in a small town in eastern Washington, I naturally gravitated toward agriculture when it came time to choose a study concentration in college. Scholarships from a wealthy benefactor helped students from my community pursue their college dreams, and, to my good fortune, I was included among them. Initially my plan was to double-major in art and biology, while slipping in a botany minor to launch me into a graduate program. As time and money grew thin, I had to quickly abandon my hopes of a formal art education. Although no longer surrounded by peers with a love of the arts, painting and drawing remained a huge part of my life. Every moment not consumed with studying chemical pathways or plant physiology was devoted to rendering my interpretations of the natural world on thick white sheets of thirsty paper. Thus began my struggle to harmoniously merge the worlds of science and art in my life. The union appealed to me, and I often used art as the security blanket which allowed me to feel at home in the scientific, "left-brained" world. I quickly began employing my creative perspective and artistic eye in oral presentations and scientific poster design. Some professors met me with intense suspicion. I was told that posters were not supposed to be pretty, that posters convey information concisely and plainly. My poster projects always morphed into interactive teaching stations, despite my best efforts to conform to the concise rules of poster design imposed by well-meaning advisers. When it came time to present to my undergraduate peers, I found the typical PowerPoint approach to be rather dreadful. I resolved to look for a better way to deliver information, even if it meant being labeled "eccentric" by my peers.

Graduate school further narrowed the social field. Surrounded by students and colleagues who were marvelously brilliant, I often felt like a foreigner immersed in a culture which lauded those rigidly analytical in their thought processes. When confined to giving PowerPoint seminars, I brought props and employed videos, audience participation, and animated clip art. My evaluations reflected the resistance to this approach. For the first time, I recognized the value and necessity of different methods of teaching. Professors who have devoted most of their lives to the study of the field preferred a direct and crisp delivery of information, devoid of anything that could even remotely be considered "frills." However, upon interacting with growers groups, community organizations, and youth, I found my interactive approach to be well received. In preparation for presentations to growers, I would make microscope slides of common pathogens that plagued their crops. Microscopes would be made available, and I loved seeing their faces as they glimpsed, for the first time, the beauty of an organism with which they had been fighting a chemical war for most of their farming careers. They would make comments such as, "It's so pretty and delicate. I have never seen it up close before. Do you have anything else on here?"

When conversing with colleagues or giving presentations to the department, however, I quickly learned to streamline and dilute my creative ideas to make them more palatable to the professional audience. While some professors were supportive, my evaluation sheets reflected consistent resistance to some of my methods. Having been raised in the age of MTV and video games, I was previously unaware there were actually people in the world who could receive too much stimuli, so I reconciled by modifying my presentation techniques appropriately.

My time as a graduate student quickly passed. Soon I found myself crossing over that thin line separating the ambitious and hopeful graduate student from the ominous "real world." Degree in hand, I entered a new phase in life, one which came complete with an office, nameplate, and the responsibility of educating individuals old enough to be my grandparents. The task to which I had been assigned, and in fact am currently working, was serving as the state coordinator of the University of Wyoming's Master Gardener Program.

The department within which I was housed had never had a female faculty member and was dominated by men. The culture of the college was strongly masculine, and a sense of cowboy independence permeated daily life. Talk of hunting, horses, pack mules, and the price of beef bonded the male members of the department. At times it certainly felt as though I was working in a foreign country, one with its unique customs, language, and culture. Being young, female, and not from a ranching background made it challenging to relate to my colleagues. My interest in the arts and relative youth seemed to cement my status as an outsider. Many members of the faculty and staff related to me within the context that they felt most comfortable and interacted with me more as they would a daughter or niece than a colleague. While this did work to instill a sense of belonging, it was notably unique and also a sign of how I would come to relate to the master gardeners in a teacher/student capacity. I only began to fully realize the challenge ahead of me when one seasoned educator pulled me aside and told me, "As a young woman, you must work twice as hard and get only half as much credit."

My daily duties consisted of resolving conflicts and overseeing routine activities within each county's Master Gardener Program. The Master Gardener Program was founded in the state of Washington in 1972. The premise behind the program was to train volunteers to assist the public with horticultural questions. Initially the volunteers are given scientifically based courses taught by Cooperative Extension Service employees and occasionally experienced master gardeners. After the training is completed, the participants are expected to repay a set number of volunteer hours working for Cooperative Extension. Volunteer activities include answering phone calls from the public, going on yard calls, maintaining community gardens, working information booths at public venues, and various other horticulture-related tasks. Every state in the nation has implemented a Master Gardener Program. The popularity of and participation in the program have grown exponentially, and the volunteer service provided by the participants is an invaluable resource for both the Cooperative Extension Service and the land-grant universities. While the Wyoming Master Gardener Program is relatively young when compared with those of more densely populated states, we maintain active groups in the following counties: Albany/Carbon, Campbell, Crook, Fremont, Goshen, Laramie, Lincoln/Teton, Natrona, Park, Sweetwater, and Weston. My charge was to strengthen and organize the program at the state level, provide training to individual county groups, maintain continuity among counties, and work toward the long-term goal of having an active Master Gardener Program in each county.

My first venue was Jackson, Wyoming, on a cold February evening. The temperature was 2 degrees Fahrenheit, to be exact. I had spent the seven-hour drive from Laramie going through the slides in my head, imagining all that could go wrong, and pounding to death those inner timorous voices. Stories about the well-educated and wealthy clientele in Jackson filled me with doubts and worries. Doctors, lawyers, movie stars, and wealthy business-people flocked to the town of Jackson to soak up the beautiful scenery and play in the abundant winter snow. This was certainly not the typical rural, friendly, and laid-back Wyoming town. I had visions of women pulling up for the Master Gardener meeting in BMWs and high heels, accompanied by their personal gardener and asking questions about how to grow price-less orchids in their million-dollar mansions. Surely I'd lose their respect when I'd admit that I grew up in a drafty trailer, hadn't the slightest clue about orchid culturing, and had never set foot in a million-dollar home or driven a BMW. As so often proves to be the case, my fears were unfounded. While the participants filed in the door, I studied their faces for clues as to their social status. Much to my surprise, most were more nervous than I about being in the class. Immediate apologies sprung out of the early arriv-als for having little experience with gardening. Several expressed concerns that they hadn't been in a classroom setting for more than twenty years. None commented on my age or even seemed to question my experience. While it was an atypical audience and a bitterly cold evening, it proved to be the typical and enduring warm Wyoming welcome.

After the meeting, I studied the evaluation sheets. The words of praise and thanks were not only palliative, they were enlivening. One participant wrote, "Raina's passion for 'botany basics' and her enthusiasm are conta-gious!" Another wrote, "I can't wait until next week!" The students also provided invaluable and constructive criticism that allowed me to gauge the number of students who were overwhelmed and the number who were very comfortable with the material. The Jackson audience proved espe-cially challenging because of the great variation in biology education and experience. Some of the participants had taken courses in botany and basic biology not long ago, whereas others had no formal biology training. Overall, I was pleased with the results of my first Master Gardener class and was resolved to improve upon my material and press on. My most

important lesson learned from this group was how essential a positive attitude and a love of teaching are when relating to students. This lesson was
certainly not lost on me.

Subsequent venues took me to Rawlins, Gillette, Afton, Riverton,
Laramie, Torrington, Evanston, and Rock Springs. As I traveled that first
year, I began to appreciate the unique flavor of each county and the Master
Gardener students there. While in Gillette, I encountered many individuals relatively new to Wyoming. Having arrived with the boom in the mineral
and gas industry, they were hoping to be able to find methods for growing
the same plants they had "back home." Rawlins consisted of folks who had
lived in Wyoming for a long time and had given gardening a try through
trial and error with varying degrees of success. Afton, with its extremely
short growing season and high-value ranchettes, drew individuals with an
interest in managing small acreages and short-season vegetable gardens.
In fact, individuals in Afton were uninterested in learning anything about
potential diseases because of the infrequency of such problems in their
area. Folks in Torrington, part of Wyoming's banana belt, actually needed
and demanded more training on diseases and disorders as they were able
to grow a wider variety of vegetables and were in closer proximity to commercial irrigated agricultural fields. As I repeated the teaching circuit in
subsequent years, I learned what special needs existed in each county and
how to prepare for discussions.

Because of my youthful countenance, I was often mistaken for a graduate student. Interestingly enough, this initial misconception did not lower their appreciation or respect. Wherever I went, I was always greeted
warmly and with approval. At times I was asked if I knew daughters or sons
attending the university. Frequently I received pre-lecture confessions of
fear and anxiety about having to learn so much information for the Master
Gardener course. I did my best to assuage doubts and instill enthusiasm.
Furthermore, in many counties experienced gardeners or professional
members of the green industry attended my training sessions. My initial
fears of being considered unknowledgeable or having the audience balk
at the rudimentary nature of the training proved unfounded. Rather, I was
able to use their great reservoir of experience, and they willingly provided
me with new ideas and innovations. Quick to admit when I was uncertain

about a question asked, these individuals often chimed in with thoughts or answers, thus contributing to the positive atmosphere of the class.

My initial year of conducting Master Gardener trainings also focused on making personal connections with the students who would hopefully become dedicated volunteers. When the group was small enough, I encouraged them to tell me their names and give the class a brief description of their gardening experience or tell why they were interested in this class. Most of the Master Gardener training occurs in a semiformal lecture format, so this was often the first time the students had an opportunity to learn about each other. While I found it nearly impossible to remember names from week to week and town to town, I did try to remember the students' special interests and take note of individuals who had recently moved to Wyoming from other states. At the beginning of each session, I took a few moments to encourage the master gardeners to write down my contact information and correspond with me whenever they had questions or concerns after the lecture. Few actually attempted to contact me, but those who did quickly became familiar with me and felt encouraged and secure in their efforts.

As I continued to make my yearly training rounds across the state, occasionally familiar faces would pop up in my classes. The previous year's students were returning to the course to hear me speak again. Most times they had heard the same information presented by me in nearly the same format. I became nervous and apologetic to this group for their need to endure a "rerun" seminar. Moreover, I became perplexed as to why they were showing up again to a beginning training. My fears were finally assuaged when I read the ever informative evaluations. One woman from Evanston who had seen me give the same presentation to the beginning Master Gardener group two years in a row wrote, "Very enjoyable! Second time and I learned a lot. I would enjoy this every year. Thank you very much!" Another second-time participant in Rawlins wrote, "I learned so much more this time around! Never be worried about second-time students in the class!" Without these valuable words of encouragement, I believe I would still feel nervous and concerned about this issue. The commitment and resolve shown by these returning students were both humbling and inspirational. Their desire to learn the information fully and provide the highest level of volunteer service set a wonderful standard for their peers.

Changing personal habits and altering ways of thinking is often difficult, even for individuals in their mid-20s. Being a classic type A personality, I often fall into the trap of attempting to cover too much information with an overly ambitious approach. Having only one opportunity to teach a group of students each year, and furthermore having these sessions confined to less than two hours in length, my desire to prepare the students to the best of my ability would often result in a mental super-saturation of the participants. Over time I learned that attempting to use every second of class time available to cram in essential tidbits of information was much less helpful than taking the time to establish a personal connection with the audience. I found that when I went a little slower, the students warmed to me and felt at liberty to ask questions and even kid me about being fast-talking and high-strung. One woman in Gillette even commented that the reason I stay so skinny is because I talk fast and never sit down. By warning the students of my idiosyncrasies beforehand and asking them to stop me if I start to pick up too much speed, the students become active participants in the effort to keep me on the right track and traveling at a moderate, but sufficient, pace. This aspect of my teaching remains my biggest challenge.

Some of my greatest encouragement and valuable rewards for my efforts have come in the form of insightful comments from experienced master gardeners. One woman, who spent her entire life as a teacher, pulled me aside after a class and said, "You are an excellent teacher." Based on all her years of experience, I was flattered and replied, "Thank you very much." She coolly retorted, "It's not meant to be a compliment; it's just a fact." Positive reinforcement keeps me inspired and excited to do my job. Both educators and seasoned master gardeners have embraced me and my unconventional teaching style, thus making the transitions in the Master Gardener Program relatively smooth and painless. I have earned the trust of my colleagues, a gift that I do not take lightly.

After holding my position as assistant coordinator for nearly three years, I developed a strong rapport with my master gardeners. Predominantly elderly and female, they looked to me not only for guidance in their program but also for friendship, reassurance, and support. Each time I ventured out to the counties to conduct additional teaching, training, and management activities, I spent at least one additional hour at each location hearing stories of new grandchildren, family illness, and personal history. Developing this unique and personal relationship with the volunteers helped to ensure the retention and success of the program. One woman even stated, "I take everything you say and etch it in stone." She was quite serious, and I smiled and told her that such action could prove very dangerous for me someday! She laughed. The enthusiasm for the program was enhanced by these personal connections and the feeling that there was somebody at the state office to whom the master gardeners could personally relate.

By acting in an administrative capacity, many of the master gardeners projected upon me the role of a counselor. One master gardener, upon obtaining my personal cell phone number, called me at home one evening under the auspice of discussing some issues about the Master Gardener Program. The phone call lasted for more than forty-five minutes, and the woman's concerns about her job were the main topic. The Master Gardener Program was discussed only briefly, and then the woman expressed self-doubt and needed reassurance that she was indeed doing a good job as a volunteer. She primarily wanted to vent about her bad day. Another woman took it upon herself to help me find a husband. She quickly began researching suitable mates for me within small towns of Wyoming and telling about their admirable qualities. To perfect her research, she would ask about my preferences. "Do you mind men with kids? How old is too old? Any particular religion? When would you like to have children? Exactly how old are you, dear? Can you ride a horse?" Other women just wanted to give me a big hug upon arrival and share pieces of their lives. When I showed up in work attire, which usually consists of a formal dress and heels, some would give me motherly pats and say, "Oh, honey, aren't you pretty? Just look at you! It's not every day we get to see a pretty lady all dressed up!" as if beaming about one of their own children. While conducting one training session, a master gardener approached me and said, "Oh, I just love those heels. Do they come in my size?" In response, three other women nodded and agreed that my high heels were very nice. Ten minutes later, I was discussing the effects of the drought on the stocking rate of local rangeland with another master gardener undergoing economic hardships. I had officially become a cowgirl in high heels. While initially some of these behaviors felt a little intrusive, I quickly learned that with this particular program and in this particular state, the personal relationship between educator and volunteer is critical. My approachability has made me very successful in my current position.

Not all interactions have been positive, however. After the initial teaching and training period passes, my role shifts from education about gardening topics to lessons in mediation and social conduct. As with any group, hurt feelings, tensions, and jealousy occur within the Master Gardener Program. I have had to mediate over half a dozen conflicts in various counties. Most fights and disagreements stem from hurt feelings. Members feel they have not been appreciated for their contributions. Others are hurt when someone else receives credit for an idea that was originally theirs. The groups of volunteers often look to the University of Wyoming for guidance and recognition. My goal as an educator then becomes to teach the volunteers how to respect and acknowledge the contributions of others. At times, I find myself in the role of judge and jury, which can be quite awkward. One Master Gardener group in conflict wanted an official letter sent to the folks on the other side of the issue emphatically stating that they were "right." Carefully I had to explain that seldom in such disagreements can one side be labeled "right" and another "wrong." These conflicts arise daily and must be dealt with sensitively.

Living and working in a sparsely populated state empowers the citizens. Everyone feels like they should and will have a voice. This firm belief, while positive and productive in most regards, can compound problems and create challenges for field educators like me. When someone becomes disgruntled with their experience as a volunteer, the very first course of action that comes to mind is speaking to the university dean personally about their problem. Few administrative buffers exist to protect educators from disgruntled citizens, and one has to learn to develop a very thick skin. I have dealt with this by starting my mediation sessions with this statement: "The goal of this mediation session is to leave here today with all of you mildly annoyed but nobody furiously angry. That's how I know

I've done my job." Everyone laughs and understands my basic struggle. I emphasize the impossibility of pleasing all people, but for some this is not enough. The same personal accessibility that makes me successful is also responsible for creating my biggest challenges. Another interesting component of the "small state" complex is everyone knows somebody who applied for your job, or your supervisor's job, or the county educator's job, but was not selected by the hiring committee. Routinely, volunteers will state, "Well, I don't think John Doe is a good educator. You know they interviewed John Brown for that position, and he would have been better." Volunteers who are well acquainted with the campus politics at times carry deep resentments, which must be carefully managed through tactful education efforts. Yet overall the volunteers approach their training and service with an open mind and willing hands, which makes my job a delight.

Drawing from and encouraged by my successes in adult education within the Master Gardener Program, I found courage to take this teaching style back into the collegiate setting populated by Ph.D.–level specialists. As mentioned above, my attempts to give interactive seminars in graduate school were met with a degree of resistance. Using newly acquired confidence and finesse, however, I tried my hand at a faculty-oriented interactive seminar on the relationship between art and science. The evening before my seminar, I covered the lights with colored spotlight film, arranged the desks by color into direct rows, and created an artificial stained-glass–window effect using overhead projectors and spotlight film shapes. Furthermore, I purchased scented markers and required ten members of the audience to draw something that the scent reminded them of. During the presentation, I passed out hands-on displays of mergers between visual arts and science. Classical music was played in short intervals as a reminder of the relationship between performing arts and mathematics. Members of the faculty commented, "We've never had anything like this before." The seminar was well received, and compliments abounded. I came to appreciate the importance of combining a receptive audience with a progressive form of education. Even the busy office associates made time to attend, and there was much buzz afterward about the nontraditional topic and presentation method. Finally I felt that I was striking a professional balance between my love of art, creative style, and unique personality. The motto of my alma mater, Central Washington University, is, "By teaching, we learn." There is much truth in that statement, for truly I was coming into my own. My experience with the master gardeners had enriched my professional career immensely.

An insatiable wanderlust and intense curiosity have led me to embark upon excursions to other parts of the world. During the cold Wyoming winters, I routinely use my vacation time to escape to warm regions, where I seek to learn about others' culture and their agricultural systems. While traveling, I always end up teaching at least one seminar. The small country of Guyana is laden with poverty but is rich with eager and ambitious youth. There I had the opportunity to speak to a group of university students specializing in tropical agriculture. In Thailand, I presented a lecture to a group of university faculty on agricultural practices in Wyoming. In both instances, my teaching skills honed in the highlands of Wyoming served me well in the equatorial jungles. Inundated with media images regarding the superiority of American agriculture, I did my best to instill hope and encourage these agriculturalists of developing countries, who in truth possessed more agricultural knowledge than I will ever aspire to. Having to rely on farming to survive makes one savvy and resourceful. The reciprocal teaching methods I found effective in the United States were even more valuable when traveling abroad. I used audience participation, encouraged discussion, drew diagrams, and focused on making personal connections instead of inundating the audience with information. The memories of these experiences in turn enriched my understanding of the world and made me a better educator back home.

Through the past five years, I have slowly learned to trust my teaching skills and agricultural knowledge. Delivering messages with a unique flair, even when going against tradition, can have wonderful results. Each opportunity I have to speak, I learn from my master gardeners and savor their wealth of knowledge and wisdom. Judging from their enthusiasm and kind compliments, I am convinced they also value the information they have learned from me. Even in this unique setting, where the teacher travels hundreds of miles to speak to an ever-changing population of students, I was able to make a contribution that strengthened this important program, which in turn enriches our communities. Despite fears, I was able to harness my distinctive talents, youthful energy, and unconventional style while delivering information that was then relayed via volunteers to hundreds of individuals who have never set foot on the UW campus. Trusting my instincts and expectations did not come easy, but come it did. The journey has been both challenging and fabulously rewarding. Through this process, I was able to form many friendships from all generations, a hidden and lasting gift that I truly had not anticipated.

As I close this essay, I am reminded of an old song that my parents used to play when I was a child:

> *Can you imagine us*
> *Years from today,*
> *Sharing a park bench quietly?*
> *How terribly strange*
> *To be seventy.*
> *Old friends,*
> *Memory brushes the same years.*
> *Silently sharing the same fears.*

("Old Friends" by Paul Simon)

References

Angelou, Maya. 1993. *Wouldn't Take Nothing for My Journey Now.* New York: Random House.

Simon, Paul. 1968. Excerpt from "Old Friends." Album: *Bookends.* New York: BMI and Columbia Records.

9

Mary Kay Wardlaw

Mary Kay Wardlaw has a B.S. in agricultural communications and an M.S. in extension from the University of Wyoming College of Agriculture. She is pursuing a Ph.D. in adult education in UW's College of Education. During her fifteen years as a county-based educator for Wyoming Cooperative Extension Service, Wardlaw worked five years in Big Horn County and ten years in Albany County. Her primary responsibilities encompassed family and consumer sciences, and 4-H and youth development. In college she learned efficient and effective ways to find and document information, as well as how to organize her work and manage time. Working in the field gave her hands-on experience in community development, adult education, and youth development. After her county work, she served four years as an education specialist for a regional health promotion and research project, where she designed community-based interventions. In 2004 she began working for the Cent$ible Nutrition Program as the education specialist, and in 2006 she became director. The Cent$ible Nutrition Program is a United States Department of Agriculture (USDA) grant-funded effort dedicated to helping low-income people "feed their families better for less." As she now works toward a doctoral degree in adult education, she draws upon twenty-plus years of experience as she reflects on and chooses to employ various educational theories and models. She is a lifelong adult learner who also welcomes opportunities to be an adult educator.

How Do You Pickle Pigs' Feet?

What Is This Education Called Extension?

A day in the life of an extension educator is never routine, boring, or without a few surprises. While I have never actually been asked how to pickle pigs' feet, as part of my job I have donned a hamburger costume, been arrested and fingerprinted, and researched how many calories are contained in the glue on an envelope flap.

When I was a 4-H member in Cheyenne, Wyoming, I dreamed of a career in extension. Those extension agents had the best job. They traveled, planned activities, and attended county and state fairs! They participated in youth events and meetings that were fun and exciting. I didn't notice they worked a lot of nights and weekends, and I never imagined they had to write so many reports, prepare grant proposals, and document effectiveness of their programs.

Now, thirty years after becoming a 4-H junior leader and twenty years after starting in extension, and in spite of all the paperwork, I believe extension education really is the best job for me. Community-based education is interesting, exciting, and challenging, and it is vital to the mission all land-grant universities, including the University of Wyoming.

Explaining the role of an extension educator is often challenging. Established in 1914 through the Smith-Lever Act, Cooperative Extension was designed as a partnership between the United States Department of Agriculture (USDA) and state land-grant universities. Land-grant universities were authorized federally by the Morrill Acts of 1862 and 1890. More recently, the National Association of State Universities and Land-Grant Colleges (NASULGC) issued a report challenging institutions to build upon the rich heritage of service and to meet new demands by becoming more engaged. They define an engaged institution as "...one that is responsive, respectful of its partners' needs, accessible and relatively neutral, while successfully integrating institutional service into research and teaching..." (NASULGC 1999, x). At the University of Wyoming, the Cooperative Extension Service is housed in the College of Agriculture. Like other extension educators, my job is to serve as part of an engaged university and share information statewide, especially new knowledge discovered through research.

Twenty years ago, as a green extension educator, this weighty task to educate the public seemed ominous. I knew the history and purpose behind my job but was unsure how to efficiently and effectively disseminate information in a large, rural county where I knew no one. The logical and appropriate first step involved working with established extension homemaker groups. Many of the county's small communities had active clubs eager for the new family and consumer sciences extension educator to show them what she had. I scheduled presentations and set out to make a difference in the world—or at least one small corner of it.

My husband, being keenly aware of Wyoming roads and weather, advised we purchase a good four-wheel-drive vehicle for my travels. The Ford Bronco II seemed to fit the bill even though it had a high center of gravity. One night I headed out in my new vehicle to find a ranch house in southern Big Horn County for my first meeting with the local homemakers' club. With my educational pump well primed, I was set to impress them with my scholarly ability to memorize information and tell them what I knew (I was a UW President's List student, after all). On the way, I had to turn right off the highway onto an unlit dirt road. I quickly discovered it was the wrong road, so I made a U-turn. Next thing I knew, my rear right wheel was in the ditch where the culvert ran under the road, and my left front wheel was off the ground. In the mid-1980s, there were no cell phones. Luck was with me, however, and before too long, a local landowner came by and stopped. He had left his house because the homemakers' club was meeting there and the new extension educator was coming. With the speed and efficiency of a skilled rancher, he had me back on the road and headed to his house in minutes. Shook up, embarrassed, and late, I was in no shape to give the lofty presentation I had prepared. But these ladies were so kind and warm. They helped me laugh about my situation and welcomed me into their club and into their lives. I discovered the people I was there to serve were bright, experienced, and mature adult learners who had a lot to teach this fresh-from-college educator.

Bad News Bearers

Research-based information may not always be good news for learners. New knowledge may require a change they do not want to make in their lives. As an adult educator in a community setting, I am aware that learners have the option of walking away and never using the information regardless of my skills, creativity, or clarity. In a traditional classroom, students are often required to complete assignments and take tests to indicate some level of learning. In extension work, it may be more challenging to require follow-through on what is taught.

Shortly after I began working as a county extension educator, a large research project on home canning was undertaken at Pennsylvania State University. A state extension specialist participated in the national training and then taught county educators the newest recommendations. I encouraged local groups to learn more by having me come to their meetings to share the latest methods. Once again, I set out to make a difference.

One of my first audiences for this program was a church group of older women who had canned food since they were young children. They learned from their mothers and grandmothers, and they taught their daughters and granddaughters. For most home-canners, the new recommendations required making major changes to their traditional techniques.

Understandably, the learners were skeptical. My level of canning experience could never match theirs. Yet I was telling them to change their techniques. They asked tough questions and vigorously challenged the information I presented. At that moment in my career, I understood the significance of research-based information as the foundation for extension education. I listened to their frustrations while not wavering from the recommendations. I explained that newer technologies can help people understand harmful bacteria and viruses in new ways and that the current recommendations were designed to ensure the safety of home-canned food.

Following the presentation, I was concerned the group felt negatively toward me or the extension program. Did they see my educational outreach effort as an embrace or as a rejection? Once again, I was reminded of the maturity and experience of these adult learners. Several ladies spoke with me and said they understood and appreciated that I was sharing important information. The real proof was when they invited me back as a presenter for their group and they promoted the canning presentation to other groups in their church.

Food safety seems to be a topic that generates interesting queries. Over the years, I have been asked if it is safe to cook in the dishwasher ("Isn't it kind of like boiling or steaming?"), how to can peanut butter, and what to do with all the food that thawed when a freezer quit working. One woman cried when I told her a food was not safe to eat and she should throw it out. Another caller said, "I knew that, but I needed someone official to tell me so I could actually throw it away."

Not all questions relate to research-based content areas. One day a lady called to say a goat had jumped into her yard and wondered if I could help identify the goat's owner. After a few phone calls, I found the owner and learned the goat, known for his escape skills, had walked more than two miles from his home. One spring I had a call asking how many calories were consumed when a person licked the glue on an envelope flap. That question I was unable to answer.

Please Don't Be Boring

After five years as an extension educator in Big Horn County, I moved to Albany County to serve in a similar position. Being home to the only university in the state, Albany County is a unique place to be an extension educator. I wanted to quickly establish myself as a resource and help create a bridge between the "ivory tower" and the community.

I soon received a call asking me to prepare a lunchtime nutrition presentation for a large group of local women. My immediate excitement waned when the caller said, "...and the ladies asked me to be sure it would not be boring. You know how most people think nutrition is boring. I assured them you would not be boring, okay?" I wondered how anything I ever had to say could be boring. If I found it interesting enough to teach, it must be exciting to the listeners too, right?

Adult education trainer and author Joye Norris (2003) champions the goal of learners leaving an educational session knowing how brilliant they are, not how brilliant their educator is. When educators activate prior learning, they begin with learners' knowledge and build from there. Norris shares, "Your role as a teacher is to find as many ways as possible for your learners to show you how smart they are" (Norris 2003, 28). Regardless of the topic, as an educator, I want learners to take with them something they can do to improve their own lives.

Norris supports a learning task model that grounds the content in the lives of learners. The model also provides for learners to do something useful with the information, reflect upon it, and transfer it into the future. It includes four As: "anchor, add, apply, and away." Typically, the learning task model is used in planning an educational session.

As an example of the learning task model, I have taught a course titled Once-a-Month Cooking. Participants learn how to prepare a month's worth of main dishes in one day. By planning, purchasing, and preparing the foods ahead, people save money and time while improving food safety and nutrition. In the classes, I first *anchored* the topic by asking participants to tell the group something they liked to cook and to describe challenges they faced in trying to regularly provide hot home-cooked meals. I then *added* new information by explaining how to use the menu plans, grocery lists, and task sheets to carry out the process. Teams of learners then *applied* this information by preparing dishes using the task sheets. During this time, more experienced cooks helped newer cooks learn food preparation techniques. As we sampled the food, we shared ideas for making mealtimes pleasant. At the end, the learners developed their own goals and shared their intent to move this plan *away* into the future to help improve their family's health through planned meals.

The learning task model can also be applied to a community educational program, such as a healthful breakfast campaign. When it comes to nutrition, most people know some of the basics such as the importance of having breakfast or more fruits and vegetables. But acting on this knowledge on a regular basis is a step people may or may not take. One year, during National Nutrition Month, the local nutrition council, which I led, promoted the importance of breakfast. The council members wanted to get people's attention and provide tools to make it easier for them to improve their health by eating breakfast more regularly and by helping them make more nutritious breakfast choices.

Since our classroom was the community, *anchoring*, or grounding, the topic of breakfast in people's lives required some creativity. We started by working with the county commissioners to develop a proclamation that they agreed to sign during a morning meeting at which we provided a sack-breakfast for each commissioner. This was publicized in the local paper. Local radio station morning talk shows offered another venue where we provided sack-breakfasts, this time for disc jockeys, while talking about the benefits of breakfast.

Strategies for *adding* new information included presentations at day-care facilities and schools, and at meetings of civic groups and organizations. Council members shared research-based information about breakfast in creative ways. For young children, we told an animated story of "Nibbles the Beaver." The children joined in, acting out Nibbles's day, seeing how he had more energy and could think better when he ate breakfast. Adult audiences received recipes and samples of quick and easy breakfast foods.

In addition to providing ideas to enhance morning meals, council members distributed a list of nonperishable breakfast foods as part of a community-wide breakfast food drive. These food items were often not available at the food banks. We offered an opportunity to *apply* (or do something with) this information by locating receptacles for donated non-perishable breakfast foods around town. We collected and weighed the food using the local port-of-entry scales. In the end, more than 450 pounds of food was donated, and, considering the weight of a box of cereal, this represented a lot of food!

In cooperation with the senior center meal-delivery program, council members prepared menus for breakfast meals. The senior center contributed staff and food for the breakfasts, and we recruited twenty-three homebound seniors to participate. Volunteers delivered breakfast to these seniors for ten days, complete with a place mat featuring research-based information supporting the value of eating breakfast.

The breakfast food drive and breakfast meal delivery provided the tools necessary to allow community members as learners to move the information into the future. This *away* component of the learning task model comes into play when individuals have a sense of self-efficacy or believe they have the ability and skills to make a change in their behavior.

A Skilled Educator as a Hamburger

In his book *Enhancing Adult Motivation to Learn: A Comprehensive Guide for Teaching Adults*, Raymond Wlodkowski shares five pillars of a motivating instructor: expertise, empathy, enthusiasm, clarity, and cultural responsiveness. He writes, "These core characteristics can be learned, controlled, and planned for by anyone who instructs adults. I see them as the five pillars on which rests what we as instructors have to offer adults" (Wlodkowski 1999, 25).

One successful community education campaign I coordinated focused on cooking ground beef to a safe temperature to kill the bacterium *Escherichia coli* O157:H7 (*E. coli*). The bacterium was making big news with the deaths of a number of people, including several young children, who ate undercooked hamburgers. I teamed up with the local health inspector, and we planned and carried out a rather unusual eight-week project. To gain *expertise*, we participated in a food-safety training in Washington, D.C., learning the most recent recommendations for preventing foodborne illnesses and learning techniques to effectively share these messages.

A key to this project was having *empathy* for people's hesitation to eat any red meat for fear of getting sick from *E. coli*. When cooked properly, meat is safe. Yet consumers' avoidance of red meat could potentially hurt the beef industry in Wyoming. Tackling this topic became an issue of cultural responsiveness as well as food safety.

Armed with sheets of thick foam from a local automotive upholstery business, yards and yards of colored felt from the discount store, and a costume pattern, I set out to *enthusiastically* show people how to cook burgers safely. A three-foot-wide hamburger costume and a pickle hat did the trick. I donned this heavy suit—consisting of a foam-and-felt bun with sesame seed buttons, burger patty, cheese and tomato slices, and a pickle spear— at many events, even the UW homecoming parade. Dressed as a hamburger, I visited schools, day-care centers, civic club meetings, grocery stores, the flu clinic, and local media outlets. Try to imagine how this looked as I am less than five feet tall. With my head as the pickle spear, I was a huge hamburger with only my feet and hands sticking out.

An important component of the costume was the enlarged version of a disposable cardboard thermometer called a T-stick. When a T-stick is inserted into the center of a completely cooked hamburger, the tip of the T-stick changes color, indicating an internal temperature hot enough to kill *E. coli* O157:H7. We obtained more than twenty thousand customized T-sticks from the manufacturer to distribute with our contact information.

Many volunteers, including local CowBelles (women involved with cattle ranching), 4-H members, and extension homemakers, assisted with the campaign, providing hands-on demonstrations at grocery stores and schools. Being involved in the teaching empowered these volunteers to help share the message, which serves as a strong motivator for learning. Many of the same volunteers helped with telephone surveys to assess the effect of the campaign.

The project had a clear, simple message: cook ground beef to at least 160 degrees Fahrenheit. At the end of the campaign, the survey indicated that in Albany County we had increased awareness of how to cook hamburger properly from 9.6 percent to 46.8 percent. This project demonstrates how extension education is more than telling people what is known through research. It is about brokering knowledge and facilitating opportunities for people to learn. It is also about creating supportive environments and providing tools for people to act on the knowledge. Our campaign garnered attention because it focused on a widely held value: the protection of families and, especially, children. It provided T-sticks as tools for immediate application, and it offered a memorable, concise message.

Community as Classroom

Adult learners are complex. They have complicated lives and many responsibilities. They enter into educational settings for a variety of reasons, usually by choice and often out of a desire to improve their lives. Traditional classroom approaches create a hierarchy where the teacher holds the knowledge and students are vessels to be filled with that knowledge to be used later. Brazilian educator and influential educational theorist Paulo Freire calls this the *banking system* of education. In contrast, for education to be most effective, adult learners need to be respected for the skills and knowledge they bring to the educational setting, and their learning must be relevant to their lives today. Freire calls this *dialogue*. This approach creates more of a partnership between the learner and the teacher and encourages listening (Vella 2002).

Being part of a local leadership program was a life-changing experience for me. I spent one year as a learner participating in monthly sessions covering community development, team building, leadership styles, and community services. As an alumnus the second year, I was part of the group responsible for planning sessions for the next class. For one such session, the topic was justice and the law. We could have brought in guest speakers, for example, a lawyer, law enforcement officer, or prison guard; however, we chose to choreograph a more realistic experience to involve the learners.

We began with a tour of the city police department. After the tour, the class boarded the local public transportation bus reserved just for our group. On our way to tour the jail, we were pulled over by a local law enforcement officer, complete with lights, sirens, and his canine partner. The officer instructed us to exit the bus. He confiscated my purse, and the police dog found "incriminating evidence" through his comprehensive (and rather aggressive) search of my purse. As I was being cuffed for transport to the jail, the class realized we had staged the event and they were going to follow along to observe the arrest and booking procedures.

At the jail, I was interrogated, fingerprinted, and photographed. The class offered some advice (one member was a lawyer), and they asked questions throughout the process. For me, even though my arrest was staged, it was nerve-racking and in many ways frightening to experience this serious situation.

Although I helped arrange this as a learning experience, I did not serve in the traditional teacher role. All members of the group were partners in this event, learning from other community members and from each other. It left a lasting impression on us, and we gained considerable appreciation for the work done by our public servants—work rarely seen by the average law-abiding citizen.

Reach Adults Through Kids

Extension youth programming, particularly the 4-H program, has a rich history in Wyoming. Extension educators realized long ago that when children learn a new skill, they often share it with their parents or other adults. Thus, teaching children is an effective way to disseminate new information throughout a community.

In Albany County, the local CowBelles group organizes an annual event called Ag Expo. They invite every third-grade class to a central location to learn various aspects of agriculture. This popular event allows the youngsters to visit booths in round-robin fashion. For several years, I hosted a nutrition-related booth focusing on protein, a nutrient found in meat products. Each ten-minute presentation started with a brief overview of how protein helps bodies grow and the kinds of food containing protein. Then, I would sit cross-legged on the concrete floor with the children, and we would slap our legs twice and clap our hands once, creating the beat of a popular rock tune. We started the chant singing, "We love, we love roast beef." Each third-grader then shouted out another kind of protein food, and we would all repeat the chant using the name of the food. The students had to quickly apply what they learned by recalling a protein food. Teachers on the buses told me the chant was sung all the way back to school. I was thrilled the students were repeating what they had learned, but I am not sure the teachers shared my enthusiasm.

Another year, I dressed in a cow costume while teaching the nutrients in dairy products. Again, the ten-minute presentation was interactive and, I hoped, somewhat memorable. After school that day, one of the third-graders accompanied her mother to the extension office for some 4-H business. I was standing in the lobby area, and as they parked the car, they saw me through the glass entryway. The little girl turned to her mother and said, "Mom, that lady is a cow." Her mother scolded her for saying something rude. "But, Mom," she insisted, "she really *is* a cow." A rather displeased mother brought her daughter into the office, unsure if she should have her apologize or pretend it didn't happen. The young girl solved the dilemma by saying to me, "Tell my mom you are a cow." The mother's shock and disapproval quickly turned to laughter as the girl and I shared the things she had learned at the Ag Expo that day. It has been nine years since this happened, and we still chuckle about it when we visit.

Learning by Doing

The 4-H motto is "learning by doing." This is also called *praxis* in adult education. *Praxis* is a Greek word meaning "action with reflection." As Jane Vella observes, "Praxis is doing with built-in reflection. It is a beautiful dance of inductive and deductive forms of learning" (Vella 2002, 115). It occurs when learners do something with new knowledge, skills, and attitudes and then reflect on what they have done. Praxis is a key element of effective adult learning and of dialogue learning. While adults may have more experience and knowledge to reflect on, I believe praxis also can have an important role in youth education. For example, consider 4-H members who gain a skill they can then share at county fair by telling and showing judges what they learned.

With rising rates of obesity in children and adults, educators worldwide are looking for ways to help people be healthier. As the education specialist for a three-state community-based health promotion project, I set out to develop an educational video for 10- to 13-year-old children, focusing on outrageous portion sizes. American youth today have grown up with 64-ounce soft drink containers and super-sized French fries. To produce an effective video, I turned to the experts for advice—sixth-grade students.

Ask a sixth-grader what to show in an educational video for other sixth-graders, and the answers include a myriad of creative, insightful concepts that are *way* outside the typical adult's thinking box. Young people feel respected and thrive when asked for their opinions and ideas. I recruited three young people from two classes to help write the script and act in the video, and, in close consultation with television production staff, I scrambled to use their creative ideas. For example, one of the segments highlighted how many sugar cubes are in a 64-ounce portion of soda pop. The young man, Otto, had read the script ahead and knew his lines. After being told an ounce of soda pop contains about the same amount of sugar as one sugar cube, he was to point to the pile of sixty-four sugar cubes and ask, "If you drink that, you would be getting this much sugar?" We had hoped he would come across as amazed or surprised, but during practice, he was simply reading the line.

While preparing for the actual shoot, he seemed distracted and fiddled with the sugar cubes. Then, suddenly, with his mouth agape, he said, "You mean, there are sixty-four of these sugar cubes in that container?" I was nearly blinded by the proverbial light bulb turning on. We changed the script so as to capture his astonishment.

These students learned some important nutrition information outside of the traditional classroom and with a dialogue approach. They were engaged in learning, they were accountable for what they learned, and they were responsible for helping make a video to share what they had learned with other young people. They took their task seriously and talked informally, off camera, about what they were learning. The actors were able to see the big picture of health promotion and the problems created by huge portion sizes. Through this knowledge and their own experiences as sixth-graders, they helped create a video that has appeal and an effective teaching message for their peers.

Lessons Learned

County-based extension education is challenging and rewarding. It provides opportunities for creative approaches to teaching and for meeting new audiences. For me, the work required that I become an integral part of my community, personally and professionally.

I sincerely believe my efforts have helped other people. Yet many people with whom I have worked have taught me more than I could ever teach them. I have learned a great deal about successful (and not-so-successful) teaching methods, gained interpersonal relationship skills, and discovered the complexity of communities. I have come to know the richness of working with adult learners who have experiences and knowledge beyond what an extension educator can ever hope to teach. I relish the excitement and unpredictable nature of youth work, often being surprised by how quickly young people learn. With responsibilities now at the state level, I draw daily upon the lessons I have gleaned from my county work and from the insights of all those people who taught me along the way.

References

National Association of State Universities and Land-Grant Colleges. 1999. *Returning to our roots: The engaged institution.* Washington, DC: The Kellogg Commission and the Future of State and Land-Grant Universities.

Norris, Joye. 2003. *From telling to teaching: A dialogue approach to adult learning.* North Myrtle Beach, SC: Learning by Dialogue.

Vella, Jane. 2002. *Learning to listen, learning to teach: The power of dialogue in educating adults,* rev. ed. San Francisco: Jossey-Bass.

Wlodkowski, Raymond. 1999. *Enhancing adult motivation to learn: A comprehensive guide for teaching all adults,* rev. ed. San Francisco: Jossey-Bass.

10
Karen Cachevki Williams

Karen Cachevki Williams has been a teacher for more than thirty years. She received her B.A. in English from the University of Illinois in 1972 and then taught high school English and French for four years in rural North Carolina. Subsequent degrees include a B.S. in family and consumer education services from the University of Wyoming in 1978, an M.A. in human development from Pacific Oaks College in 1987, and a Ph.D. in curriculum and instruction with an emphasis in early childhood education from the University of Wyoming in 1993. In addition to teaching high school students, Williams has taught infants, toddlers, preschoolers, junior high students, and college students. She developed the Department of Family and Consumer Science's online bachelor's degree program in child development in 1999. Williams's passion for travel is continually indulged not only in the United States but also with international trips to France, England, Italy, Switzerland, Germany, Canada, Mexico, Australia, and the People's Republic of China. During her sabbatical leave, she traveled around the nation to interview eighteen of her distance bachelor's degree students. Williams returned from sabbatical to take on the role of department head in June 2003.

Listening to Learn: Growing as a Teacher-Learner

I've been an educator for more than thirty years, and I can't remember a time when I didn't want to be a teacher. I have been fortunate to have worked with many age groups from infants to adults. Each age group has touched me differently. All have shaped the teacher I am today. All have touched me in ways they can never imagine.

My belief is that it's important to listen to those we teach—really listen. In my career, I've tried to hear the questions behind the questions. I use the questions to guide curriculum development, personalize instruction, help students connect to difficult content, and deepen learning. Most importantly, I use the questions behind the questions to grow as a teacher.

Curriculum Development

Do my knowledge and experiences matter? Do you value what I want to know?

When Matthew, age 4, asked me, "Do teachers go to Heaven?" I took a deep breath, prepared for the birth, death, and infinity questions 4-year-olds frequently ask. I replied, "Why do you want to know?" He sighed deeply and then responded, "Well, when you die, I want you to know that I'll take care of Melinda." Melinda was one of the dolls I used in class to be sure all underrepresented groups were visible. She was blind.

Matthew was drawn to Melinda and would hold her zipped in his jacket when we went on walks and field trips, talking to her so she wouldn't miss anything. He had loved it when Melinda first came to circle time as part of a discussion, launching the children and me into a new exploration. Melinda (she told the children through me) wondered if she could come to our school. The children had many concerns and questions. How would she see the books I read each day? Eat snacks? Participate in clean-up? Couldn't the doctor just make her better?

The questions and activities went on for weeks. Matthew's questions let me know that he wondered if I trusted him. He wanted to know what I valued. He wanted to contribute to our curriculum, to see what I would do next in class.

Jesse was like that too. His question, "Your skin color is darker than mine, isn't it?" sent us all on a wonderful exploration of families, skin color, and respect for each other. His question let me know he was trying to understand the primary colors he was learning and wondering why the words for skin color didn't fit. He and I weren't white—Elmer's Glue was white! His question let me know I would do something with his wondering. I went home that night, searching through my cupboards for good-tasting foods that were the same shades as each of my persona dolls. I brought them to class on a covered tray, sharing Jesse's question with my group of 4-year-olds at circle time. We looked at each doll, then at each food: crackers, pink grapefruit, carob, bananas, apricot applesauce, dark chocolate, and more. I still treasure the video of the children's excited explorations of their own skin color and follow-up activities on families to help children understand that we get our skin color from our parents, and that it doesn't wash off.

Young children are interested in so many things! It's one of the great joys of teaching that age group. So how should one include them in the decisions made regarding curriculum? Emergent curriculum—responsive curriculum that flows from the interests and questions of the students and their teacher—is the answer.

One strategy I used was to closely observe the individual children by noticing what they chose to play with, what they chose to collect, where they spent most of their time, what their favorite books and stories were, and their conversations with each other and their parents. I could then come to group time saying, "I notice that several of you seem curious about bees and other insects. Is that true?" I'd then start by putting *Bees* in a circle on chart paper. I'd ask the children what they wanted to know about bees, what they wondered. Each child's ideas were written in different colors so they could see that I valued their input, even though they couldn't read yet. Each idea would form a new circle, connecting to *Bees,* forming a connected web. They knew we could have more than one major exploration going on at the same time if there were multiple interests, and explorations could be pursued as long as new questions and interest arose. There would be no forced learning. "This week's topic is clowns, like it or not." And they learned to trust that we were *partners* in the best sense of the word.

Working with young children like Matthew and Jesse and using the preceding method led me to write "What Do You Wonder?" in 1997. The article discussed the importance of observing and listening to children, then building on their questions and interests by finding out what they wanted to know and learn about, what they already knew about the topic, and then what students and teachers could contribute to the exploration. I was part of the class, too, and my ideas and expertise helped bring in concepts they might not have thought of while incorporating skill building based on individual children's needs. My belief is that curriculum should be co-constructed (developed jointly by the teacher and students) if we really want it to be relevant and lead to deeper learning and processing. Emergent curriculum acknowledges up front that, though the teacher has knowledge and experience in a content area, students at every level should be respected for the knowledge and experiences they bring to the classroom. In that way, teachers are learners, and learners become teachers.

It was only natural, then, that I would extend the use of emergent curriculum and group planning meetings to my college classes. This is a challenge in academe, where one must order textbooks four to six months in advance, turn in complete syllabi before the first day of class, make sure courses are articulated at the community college level, and deal with common assessments when teaching endorsements are involved. But I knew I could take what I had learned from teaching young children. Good teaching is good teaching, learning is learning, respect for the learner is respect, no matter what age the learner. And I had, after all, been a product of the late sixties and early seventies when one followed a *teaching as a subversive activity* philosophy. For me, that meant doing what is best for students, what is supported by research, and what fits my ethical beliefs while still meeting standards and requirements.

I start every college class by asking the students what they hope to know more about or learn how to do in my course, as well as what they find already familiar. Why did they enroll in the course? What did they hope would be part of the course content? What questions did they have that they thought the content could address? What previous experiences could they bring to the table? What could we build upon in their prior learning? I write all of the questions and issues raised on the white board.

In my distance-learning classes, the questions are part of an initial intake survey and opening threaded discussion. I have never had students fail to respond, but just saying "pass," staying silent, or indicating in a distance course that one is not comfortable responding are all perfectly acceptable. Once the first one or two students comment and others see that I'm genuinely interested in what they have to say and will really incorporate their ideas, others respond.

Next, I hand out the syllabus with a tentative schedule for the course. I give them time to read it, and see if their interests seem to be covered. We talk about any questions they might have about the topics and readings. Then they take it home to ponder for a week. This gives those who weren't ready to contribute a chance to have input and really think about the course. We make any final adjustments; the syllabus is set. However, I continue to have the schedule say *tentative,* letting the students know up front that I will adjust due dates, readings, and activities based on what I'm observing in class and feedback from the formative evaluations I conduct twice during the semester. Any time I make a change, and I try not to do those so often it becomes confusing for them or me, I let them know exactly why. This follows another belief of mine: students deserve to know the reasoning behind curricular decisions. They may not always agree with the decisions, but at least they know my thinking.

Emergent curriculum strategies aren't the only ones I use that stem from student questions. It's equally important to help students learn how to pose questions for investigation. When I taught Child Development, I created a final assignment that let students pose a research question that could be explored through observational methods in the laboratory portion of the class, where students spent two hours per week in our early childhood programs. I gave a general lecture on how to form researchable questions, showing good and bad examples for discussion. Students posed questions early in the semester, then got individual feedback from me to help narrow and focus their questions to fit within the semester-long time frame. In this way, students from a wide variety of majors could do the four required observations while using information from them and from their observation notes to answer their questions. Allowing students to pursue questions of their own connects them in important ways to the course content. Students also learned some basic research techniques. Examples of their questions included:

Does age of child affect the choice of where they choose to play and explore materials? Is personal interest or the presence of friends the strongest influence?

Do 3- to 5-year-old girls interact with other girls more than they interact with boys during play and snack times? If so, is the interaction different between girls and girls, and girls and boys?

Are children from the ages of 3 to 5 capable of bias and discrimination toward each other?

Will 4-year-old children adjust their vocabulary and intonation based on the developmental level of those with whom they are conversing?

The students' final reflective assessment papers showed that they had a new understanding of data gathering and analysis as well as developmental norms. They were pleased to be able to answer, or begin to answer, a question that was of interest to them.

Diversity

Will you respect my beliefs? Is this a safe place for me to grow?

Being a white teacher and a Yankee, as I was often reminded—a foreigner in a school that was 45 percent black in the rural South—stretched me. I was only 21 in 1972, and my first teaching job was in Angier, North Carolina. Many times I tried to listen to the question behind the question. One student said, "Linda asked me not to tell you, but she's taken a bottle of aspirin. She's pregnant and really scared. What should I do?" The real question was, "Will you help me? I don't want to break her trust, but I can't help her alone. If I trust you, what will happen to me and to her?" Another student, Sandra, surprised the biology teacher and me with her cultural and folk beliefs, saying, "Well, don't you know that if you hold a snake over a fire, its back legs will pop out?" and "You're not going to make me do the film project in English class, are you? My momma told me having a picture taken captures your soul!" I got a quick lesson that wasn't part of my teacher education preparation in how to respect a student's beliefs while still teaching the curriculum. My response of, "It sounds like your family believes that photographs and videos shouldn't be taken, while others believe that they help capture and record events and people so that they can be remembered. How can we help you meet the intent of the assignment?" was modified and used more than once as I learned to teach in a respectful way.

Sometimes one makes the decision to directly challenge thinking and beliefs. As a new assistant professor, I was advised by some to avoid controversial topics and teaching strategies. I was told to wait until I had tenure. Of course, I ignored the advice. Good teaching means taking risks. Consequently, I developed Multicultural Influences on the Young Child during my first year in a tenure-track position, and have taught it ever since. The course is an antibias curriculum course that focuses on building respect for diversity and integrating multicultural strategies as essential components of teaching young children and working with families. The course looks at all the forms of prejudice that can block children's success in school and society as part of a broad definition of multiculturalism: sexism, racism, ageism, sexual orientation, sizeism, classism, ethnocentrism, language differences, handicapping conditions, and religious differences. At least one of these topics will prove to be uncomfortable for every student. Situations where one must grapple with new or uncomfortable information are essential for learning to occur. I feel it is a necessary part of the higher education experience, just as it is for very young children's learning and growth.

Creating an environment where students know it is safe to take risks is important in any classroom. It is essential in courses that deal with controversial topics. In this class, there are ground rules: it is all right to challenge ideas but not to attack an individual or his or her beliefs. Evidence in discussions and written work needs to come from readings and other published research, not just from one's opinions. However, bringing in personal experiences is permitted and encouraged as a means of stimulating discussions. I model for them, sharing my family and cultural background stories as well. In addition to the opening brainstorming session to find out what students want to know or learn how to do, I also ask the students to write anonymously on a card: What are your hopes for this class? What is your biggest fear? Surprisingly, they tell me. This continues throughout the year with sporadic feedback cards collected at the end of the class period where students let me know what was comfortable, uncomfortable, clear, or confusing about a particular topic or class. In these ways, students begin to develop a sense of trust in me and in each other.

Trusting each other and learning to respect differing perspectives is an important piece of every course I teach. In every group of students, there will be those with different learning styles. This is particularly evident when one looks at who talks, who doesn't, who is more comfortable writing than speaking, and so forth. While a useful strategy may be to allow students to self-select into small groups for discussions and activities, another strategy is to be more purposeful in how the groups are formed. In my World Literature for Curriculum Integration course (one that I only got to teach once!), I first came up with a strategy to make sure all students interacted with every member of the class. Each week I would have "provocations" set up in class. These were either thought-provoking questions for discussion stemming from the readings, activities set up on different tables, a poem or image on an overhead, or a small group task. A large folding card on each table displayed the names of the group members for that day. These changed weekly so students worked with different individuals. A recorder and facilitator were assigned; these roles also shifted weekly so everyone experienced each role. The facilitator's main role was to be sure everyone had the opportunity to contribute. The technique ensured all questions and answers weren't flowing through me while helping each student become a better listener, better communicator, and better sharer of knowledge and experiences. It also allowed me to move among groups as a listener to gauge understanding of key concepts while simultaneously being a learner.

Just as all learning doesn't take place in the classroom, all content knowledge can't come from the instructor. I can provide readings and share experiences, but I can't know what it's like to be lesbian, Latina, Muslim, homeless, or paraplegic. For students to really understand diversity, they need to ask questions of those who have those lived experiences. For preschoolers, this means inviting family members in to share their cultures and experiences and letting children with handicapping conditions be the experts to teach the others. For example, in my preschool class a child had a cleft palate and a brain shunt. Children were afraid of her because of the way she looked. She and her family brought in her photo album, using it to talk about her birth and surgeries, allowing children to ask any questions they had.

At the college level, I arrange for guest speakers or panels to come to class and have students prepare questions for them in advance to think through the deeper issues and find a way to voice them. In Later Childhood and Adolescence, I brought in UW students from many countries to share their cultures' values, rites of passage, and their own personal experiences. Students asked them such questions as: How does dating work in your country? What is schooling like for adolescents? Can everyone attend school? What is the driving age, and who is allowed to drive? Are there differences in expectations for males and females? What is parenting like?

In Multicultural Influences on the Young Child, I frequently invited members of the Lesbian, Gay, Bisexual, Transgendered Association (LGBTA) to class. Students would ask: When did you first know you were homosexual? How were you treated by your families? Your classmates? What are your goals for the future? Do you want to get married and have a family? What does a relationship mean to you? Students need to really believe there are no stupid questions, and the only way to get accurate information and not make assumptions is to ask real questions.

Distance Education

Who will be my lifeline? Will you know me and care about who I am? Is this curriculum for real?

In 1990 I was invited to be one of the first ten "Online UW" instructors. I thought it was the craziest idea I had ever heard! How could someone like me teach online? Learning was hands-on, active, responsive, and it relied upon social interactions, didn't it? But Judy Powell, then associate vice-president for academic affairs and dean of the Outreach School, convinced me to give it a try—me who could barely turn a computer on and who thought HTML might be the name of a new rock group. Within only a few years, I was sold on its benefits and initiated an online degree program.

In 2001 I attended an "inVISIBLE College" conference put on by the UW Ellbogen Center for Teaching and Learning. During one of the workshops, we discussed *The Social Life of Information* by John Seely Brown and Paul Duguid. It not only made me think about the new ways information is transmitted in the twenty-first century, but it made me question what the computer age might be doing to the social fabric of our world. I also remembered an earlier conference on campus that explored the concept of how to connect new students to each other and the campus: creating learning communities. I felt a sense of panic! I had created a distance-degree program to help place-bound women meet their career goals, thinking this was a good thing. I left the conference knowing that I had to apply for a sabbatical leave to explore the questions: How do students in the distance bachelor's degree program experience distance education? Are we creating a community of learners?

I spent the 2001–02 academic year flying around the country conducting interviews in ten different locations. I visited eighteen amazing women in their homes and workplaces. We sat together at their computers so they could show me how they approached their online courses. I met their families and co-workers. They shared their lives and their stories, and each woman was amazed that I came and cared enough to ask them what was working and not working for them, what their supports and barriers were, and about their unique experiences. These women in early-childhood settings were extremely motivated to learn, but not just because of the changing requirements for their jobs. One woman put it this way:

> So anyway, I found you on there and the whole idea was, is, that I went out with my husband and explained to him that I had to have something that was mine. You know, I loved what I was doing and where I was at, and was content that way, but I wanted something that even if it was late at night I could go on and have my own little thing that I could get away from. The house has to be redone every day, and you know, parenting and being a wife, and all that stuff. I wanted to have another something that was mine.

Connectivity was a theme that emerged from the interview data. I found students did feel connected to their adviser, faculty in our department, and the students in the online courses. They felt very disconnected in correspondence-study courses or courses they labeled "fake online courses," where they only had readings and tests but no chats, online discussions, presentations, or group work. I was heartened to know that in our online degree program, we were creating a community of learners. Here are some examples of their feelings:

The online course is much more like sitting in a classroom. It's much more. I feel I know these people and they pop back up in different classes and not unlike at a community college when you walk in and you see people that you recognize, that you know you've seen before. So I get a lot more interaction, of course, from the online courses than the flexible enrollment.

There's a gal in Georgia that keeps coming up in my classes and her husband's in the military. And so we talk [e-mail] all the time even when we're not in courses together…it's just a lot of fun to find other people that are interested in instructing and learning and just another facet of life.…And so I enjoy that, that gives a feeling of community, of actually going to college and actually being connected with the University of Wyoming. Yeah, that makes all the difference in the world.

I like the chat rooms…you get to see what other students are doing. Not only where they're from. That part's interesting, but what they're doing [professionally] and the fact that you can communicate with each other [is more so]…the suggestions and the feedback that we were giving each other as students, not only for the course, but in our work, in our jobs.

I would say I've felt more connected [than isolated]. I couldn't have felt any more connected than I would have in the classroom with other students. You know, you see them for an hour or two, and everybody goes their own way. On the contrary, I think more connected because there were times when we were in a chat, or through your threaded discussions it was a little more personal information in there that maybe in the classroom I would not have gotten.

I love that people are all over the world. I think that's wonderful. I don't want to know about what's being done here locally because I work here locally and I know most of that. You know, I want to know what everybody else is doing in New York, in Wyoming, you know not even the Head Start programs, just with early childhood.

You know, there are definitely instructors that are kind of more personable with the students. You want to know about their family life and stuff like that, whereas other instructors are kind of just like "do your work and get it done," and I tend not to remember their names either.

Stretching to learn was another theme, as was juggling. They were juggling work, children with handicapping conditions, mononucleosis, miscarriages, husbands in the military gone for long periods of time—one even did her homework at the hospital while her husband received chemotherapy each Saturday. But every one of them felt the learning and growth were worth it, even if it stretched their thinking and their skills:

So, it's a stretch for me. I must say that I always thought of my situation as being the norm. Of course, I think probably everybody does. And all these classes make me think about that maybe we aren't the norm. Maybe norm is not the right word, but there are so many situations and so many different factors that go into people and how they parent and how they deal with their children that I never even considered. It's just way out in left field for me. We've done a lot of different things with a lot of different families, but they've been right here for the most part, or had roots right here. To think about inner city families and urban families and what they cope with and all that...it's completely different.

...Sometimes they don't understand that a lot of those students are nontraditional students. Because like on the flexible enrollment class again, she'd ask us to document, which is fine, but I went back to footnoting, that's all I knew and she didn't say to do anything else. So then I get back this big, long, red note saying, "Footnotes have been passé for a decade, please use MLA." Well, I didn't know. Nontraditional students may not have taken an English class for some time. We don't know that the things have changed, so all that kind of needs to be put up front so that people know.

> *Like in this case right now I have a class with a student. I knew her from before, had worked with her on a group project before in another class and knew she would do her part. Group projects are stepping outside of the box for me. Because I have to allow other people to have control. And that's not easy for me, especially control over my grade. I mean, that's where you learn how you're going to approach this person. It takes a lot of communication. I think that's one thing I underestimated was the amount of communication writing wise.*

It's no wonder that so many strove to create comfort zones by taking exams in pajamas with a mug of coffee or cocoa, placing their computers in rooms where they could stay part of their children's activities, or printing and highlighting lectures and assignments to put in notebooks just like they had done years before in face-to-face classes. Their feedback has been shared with other educators at national conferences and in articles, used to modify teaching strategies in our degree programs, and used to shape my research.

Advising

Is this my academic home?

Advising may be the favorite part of my job. Over the past fifteen years, I've advised between twenty and sixty students per semester in child development, and since becoming a department head, I meet at least briefly with every prospective student. I really see advising much as I saw working with preschool children. The essence is to create a climate of trust, encourage questions and explorations, and recognize that bumpy transitions lead to growth. Unlike Peter, the 4-year-old who emphatically wanted to be an underwater paleontologist, everyone doesn't have a clear vision of the future. In the Department of Family and Consumer Sciences, most of our students don't find us during their first year in college. Some are transfer students from community colleges or out-of-state universities. Others begin in a different department on campus or are undeclared majors. Students find the department in many ways, including word of mouth, searching the Internet, taking a course, or meeting me or a faculty member.

It's more important to have a student find the right department and a path to reach their career goals than it is for the student to choose the Department of Family and Consumer Sciences. When a student comes to my office, many times the first statement is, "I love children." I ask them to tell me their experiences with children. What is it that they love about working with children? What age group? If they could name their ideal job, what would it be? Do they see themselves as a teacher of young children in a classroom setting? Do they see themselves working with children and families in a nonclassroom setting? I listen carefully to their answers, then tell them about programs on campus that might meet their needs. If the student is changing majors, I ask why they want to change. What wasn't working for them? What might have worried them? I'm careful to stay positive about all of the departments and programs on campus, pointing out their strengths, so that if a student decides to make a change, it's for reasons that will lead to future success. I hope the student is moving toward something that excites them, not just away from something that felt temporarily uncomfortable.

Advising distance students is probably the greatest challenge for me. They are goal-driven and enthusiastic, often saying that they had been looking for an accredited online degree program for a very long time. At the same time, they frequently have conflicting expectations. They want to get their degree quickly but want to only take a course or two per semester. They want to be sure that everything they take counts for the degree but are confused about graduation requirements and differences between upper- and lower-division credits. They want to feel connected to the adviser and department but often ignore advice or fail to seek it altogether. Over the past ten years, Sarah Lee, Diana Currah, and I (all program advisers to the distance students) have tried to answer their questions, reinforce policies, bolster their self-confidence, and help them negotiate the degree maze using e-mails, phone calls, and a very occasional face-to-face visit. Yet several times distance students have traveled to Laramie for graduation (from Georgia; Washington, D.C.; Montana; California), telling us they wanted to finally see the campus and meet their adviser in person.

The hardest things about advising on-campus students are (a) finding the line that separates advising from psychological counseling, (b) balancing genuine caring with professional objectivity, (c) being helpful without doing all the work and making decisions for the student, and (d) letting students know you are available between registration sessions without letting advising take up so much time it interferes with the other parts of the job.

Let me share Ginger's story. Ginger isn't her name, but then confidentiality is an important part of advising. (One thing I don't miss about teaching in the public school is the teacher's lounge conversations where everything was shared in the open in ways I felt were unethical: students' names, family secrets, student labeling, victim blaming.) I had been Ginger's adviser for two years. Trust built up slowly as she came to my office just to say hello and share things going on in her school and personal life. She had taken my Multicultural Influences on the Young Child course, but even before then she came out to me. Maybe it was the magnet on my door with the green circle enclosing a pink triangle that showed I'd been through SAFE Zone training and would be a respectful listener. Later, trust allowed me to ask her about problems I was seeing in her writing. I suspected dyslexia. I gently approached her about her learning disorder and found the funds to get her tested so she could receive services. As with several other advisees over the years, I went with her to her first appointment at her request, helping her overcome the feeling of being labeled and misunderstood that had permeated her public-school years.

Students continue to teach me. Their questions constantly keep my teaching fresh and new, even when I've taught the same course ten times. The course can never be exactly the same as it was the previous time, nor should it, because the students are different. As I listen to their questions and try to hear the question behind the question, I'm pushed to be a questioner myself. How did things go in class today? Can I create a case study that will get at that concept better? Am I expecting too much, or too little, at this course level? Am I sharing too much of my own stories and not listening enough to theirs? The questions are endless, challenging me to be an *educator* in the very best sense of the word.

References

Brown, J.S., and P. Duguid. 2000. *The social life of information.* Boston: Harvard Business School Press.

Jones, E., and J. Nimmo. 1994. *Emergent curriculum.* Washington, DC: National Association for the Education of Young Children.

Kramarae, C. 2001. *The third shift: Women learning online.* Washington, DC: AAUW Educational Foundation.

Nimmo, J. 1997. Creating community in the classroom: Play and emergent curriculum. Early Childhood Institute, June 18–20, 1997; Laramie, Wyoming.

Piaget, J. 1985. *The equilibration of cognitive structures: The central problem of intellectual development.* Chicago: University of Chicago Press.

Shapiro, N.S., and J.D. Levine. 1999. *Creating learning communities.* San Francisco: Jossey-Bass.

Williams, K.C. 1997. What do you wonder? Engaging children in curriculum planning. *Young Children* 52(6):78–81.

11

William R. Jolley

W illiam Jolley grew up on a dryland farm in southeastern Idaho, completed K–12 schooling in the public school system in Idaho Falls,
volunteered for the U.S. Army draft (1954–56), and entered Utah State
Agricultural College (USAC) in Logan after completion of his army term.
At USAC, now Utah State University of Agriculture and Applied Sciences
(USU), he majored in civil engineering for two years, switched to zoology,
completed a B.S. degree in 1967, and then entered graduate school and
completed an M.S. degree in 1969 with research on coccidial parasitosis in
cattle. He completed a Ph.D. program at Brigham Young University (BYU)
with research projects in coccidial excystation physiology, and entered a
postdoctoral program at the University of Illinois at Urbana-Champaign
(UIUC) in the College of Veterinary Medicine, conducting research on
the effect of sewage sludge digestion on viability of parasitic protozoa and
worms. In July 1975, Jolley joined the University of Wyoming faculty in
what was then the Department of Microbiology and Veterinary Medicine,
College of Agriculture. He currently teaches Veterinary Parasitology during fall semesters and Medical Parasitology during spring semesters in
what is now the Department of Veterinary Sciences. He also supervises the
diagnostic sections of parasitology and clinical pathology at the Wyoming
State Veterinary Laboratory, which is a component of the department.

Teaching with Tales

Rambling to a Profession

Looking back on thirty-eight years of fascination with the world of parasitic worms, protozoa, and bugs, I continue to wonder why and how some of my early whimsical decisions led me to the indoor and outdoor arenas of learning and teaching parasitology. As a freshman engineering student at Utah State Agricultural College (USAC), now Utah State University of Agriculture and Applied Science (USU) in Logan, I realized within two years that my brain would become parched and useless before graduation unless I changed direction.

A switch from engineering to premedical biology sparked my interest and stimulated enough enthusiasm to enable me to complete a bachelor of science degree in zoology. An early intention to apply for admission to medical school was dropped after interviewing two local medical doctors, who confessed to me that their professional and personal lives belonged to patients and schedules and that, except for the income and some of the personal interaction with patients and co-workers, they frequently regretted being medical practitioners because of a lack of "freedom."

General Parasitology was one of my last courses for completion of the bachelor's degree. The professor who taught the course, Dr. Baylor, was a senior faculty member, very well organized and obviously interested in the subject and in us, the students. Much of what he delivered in lecture was boring taxonomy, but the gory aspects of infection with some of the protozoa and worms were riveting. He made it clear to us that the organisms we were talking about were all around, as well as frequently in, us and our pets, all of whom served as hosts. Curiously, many of us in the class noticed that he seldom appeared in our parasitology lab, where, with coaching from a graduate student we frequently dissected worms, arthropods, and animals, or processed feces or blood, looking for worms and their eggs, and protozoa and their cysts. When asked about his avoidance of lab, he admitted having a dangerous allergy to certain worms, which caused a life-threatening respiratory reaction if he was so much as present inside a room where the worms were exposed to the air that he needed to breathe. That was a graphic lesson most of us remembered clearly, and continue to associate with intestinal roundworms that are common in people, pets, and agricultural animals. The significance of that incidentally learned, personal medical problem as learning and teaching enhancement was not fully appreciated until I entered the classroom as an instructor.

My first teaching experience occurred during my senior year at Brigham Young University in a doctoral program in parasitology. Basic Zoology for undergraduate students was taught there every semester as a course so large that graduate students were assigned to teach one or more lecture sections, each containing one hundred to two hundred students. The classrooms were well equipped with then-modern instructional and sound equipment. I soon noticed that many of the students in my section tuned out the basic information I tried to deliver. If I injected a graphic association between an animal or an animal's organ system and a disgusting parasite or other damaging agent or event, most of the drowsy individuals would snap out of their trancelike state and regain focus. Some also seemed to enjoy being asked questions relative to their own experiences and knowledge of the subject. Discussion was limited due to the amount of material that had to be covered in a short period of time, but the material clearly stimulated interest in most of the serious students. That teaching experience, my first, was very time- and effort-consuming yet somehow personally stimulating, satisfying, and rewarding.

The Professional Homesite

My next teaching experience began three years later when I joined the Department of Microbiology and Veterinary Medicine at the University of Wyoming. My teaching responsibility included Diagnostic Parasitology every spring semester and Protozoan Parasitology, offered every second spring semester. Diagnostic Parasitology was then required of nursing and microbiology students, and included students in other fields of biology as an option. Enrollment was considered large, with thirty to forty students each spring semester. Protozoan Parasitology was a graduate-level course with a student enrollment of five to ten.

Current offerings in parasitology are Medical Parasitology during spring semester and Veterinary Parasitology during fall semester. Medical Parasitology is also provided to medical students in the WWAMI

(Washington, Wyoming, Alaska, Montana, Idaho) medical education program as part of a course in which medical students are introduced to parasitic, viral, and bacterial pathogens during their first year in the program.

The structured, classroom delivery of parasite-related information and discussion with students on campus probably equals the two-way learning that occurs on the phone at the Wyoming State Veterinary Laboratory (WSVL) and in meetings with producer groups, pet owners, ranchers, veterinarians, medical professionals, biologists, and random individuals. In those random discussions and meetings, I have learned as much or more about practical aspects of parasitism, or imagined parasitism, of humans and the animals they associate with, than from any textbooks, scientific articles, or research projects. In return, I have had the satisfaction of providing information and diagnostic services that enable people to better understand and manage their parasite-related "problems."

The Subject

The biology of parasites is similar to that of almost all other animals and infectious organisms, and must be understood for "we students" to accept the fact that all animals, and we personally, are subject to invasion by, and hosting of, the agents. The anatomy, terminology, life stages, relationships, damage capabilities, and distributions of the agents are basic, sometimes boring aspects of parasitology, similar in some ways to bacteriology and virology. The subject soon becomes personally applicable or exciting when someone is aware of another person or beloved animal with whom they are associated, which has been infected or affected by a parasite. Dr. Baylor's allergy to certain roundworms has turned out to be the "tip of an iceberg" of memorable, if not unforgettable, examples of experiences with parasites that can be used to horrify, fascinate, and thereby educate students, including myself.

Many people are aware of some of these invasive creatures but seldom know how common and medically or commercially important they are. In classroom discussion with students; casual settings with friends, relatives, and others; and on the phone with veterinarians, medical personnel, and numerous other individuals, it has become obvious to me that parasitology touches many, if not all, people, including those of us in "cold," relatively sterile geographic zones. Through these contacts, my knowledge of the subject has increased dramatically, and has enabled me to more effectively pass on and exchange information with others.

The "parasites" include roundworms, flatworms, single-celled protozoa, and arthropods. They depend on one or more host animals for survival and may sometimes, but not usually, cause noticeable damage, disease, or death. The significant difference between parasites and pathogenic bacterial and viral agents is the tendency of the bacteria and viruses to often kill or seriously sicken a recently infected host, unless overcome by the host's immune system or a drug treatment. Parasitic infections are more likely to be long-term, subclinical relationships that seldom threaten the life of a host. Their existence depends on an ability to develop through several complex, mandatory stages, consume nourishing nutrients from their hosts, reproduce, and pass from one host to another.

A requirement organisms must possess to qualify as parasites is an ability to damage their hosts to some degree, without which they are considered commensals of little or no medical importance. Each type of parasite has adapted to a specific environmental niche in a host's body, from the skin to the deepest visceral organs. Food requirements depend on their sites of residence in the host's body and may include tissue cells, blood, feces, or other nutritional substances. Some cause anemia, whereas others depress the immune system or initiate the development of cancer; others cause so little injury they are ignored or unnoticed. Their seriousness frequently depends on the age, health, and condition of the infected host, the size of the parasite population in the host, and the inherent ability of the parasite to damage a host.

Subject Transmission

Most people with farm or ranch experience where domestic animals are raised are aware of various worms and arthropods that parasitize their animals, simply because many of the creatures are large enough to be easily seen when passed in feces or crawling on skin. Hunters, slaughterhouse workers, butchers, and others who enter the interior, anatomical zones of animals are also "introduced" to parasitic agents in tissues and organs during evisceration or meat processing. Most people in cool, temperate areas hear about parasitic events only in an occasional magazine feature, newspaper article, or science video on TV. Consistently these accounts are written or shown for their dramatic or promotional effect. The shock value of watching Dr. House, of the *House* TV series, extracting a 25-foot-long fish tapeworm from the small intestine of a conscious, screaming young woman with pernicious anemia cannot be underestimated. Other examples of common attention-getters designed to attract viewers, readers, or shoppers include the huge, capitalized questions on the front of a magazine for "women on the go": "ARE PARASITES MAKING YOU FAT?", "NEWS: 1 IN 3 AMERICANS ARE AFFECTED."

Fortunately, most educational institutions with quality training programs in human and veterinary medicine provide infectious-disease courses that include parasitology. Teaching veterinary parasitology differs little from that of medical parasitology in basic biology, identification, and control of infectious agents, but the fear factor that enhances memory retention is more easily produced in the medical area. Whereas veterinary parasitology is interesting and economically important, it is not as personalized and stressful as being personally identified as a host for a pinworm, tapeworm, or diarrhea-causing intestinal protozoan, especially if the agent was acquired locally in a cool climatic area where the organisms are not "common." Travelers are frequently cautioned about infectious agents commonly acquired in foreign destinations, but many people, including medical professionals, are unaware of risks in our local residential and recreational areas. Medical doctors in tropical and subtropical areas are much more likely to be aware of and test a patient for a parasitic agent than are MDs in cool, temperate regions, unless they have personally dealt with a parasitized patient or have had the opportunity to serve patients in a climatic zone with significant parasite presence.

Classroom teaching is the most efficient and satisfying method of passing parasitology on to others, though it is sometimes challenging and difficult. Students differ in personality characteristics, both individually and as a group. Some student groups are participative, interested, and consistent, whereas others may be somewhat shy and reluctant to participate in discussions. Every class I have taught has had a number of bright, interested students with strong motivation to learn the subject or achieve a high grade. Reaching and stimulating even those motivated to succeed sometimes requires tweaking methods that have been effective with previous groups. Some respond willingly to questions asked at the beginning of a lecture, for example, while others need to be "warmed up" by a short review of recent discussion material or an illustrative story about a parasitized resident human, pet, or game animal. Within a few minutes after the beginning of a class period, the current mood of the group can usually be sensed, enabling me to instinctively proceed with a more or less riveting case description that leads into the day's subject material. These techniques are especially effective in classes with two or more "nontraditional" students, usually older (more seasoned) than the average undergraduate. The nontraditional students are consistently less shy than their younger classmates and are more likely to ask questions, discuss issues, show more enthusiasm, and unconsciously provide a lift in the interest and attitude of the entire group. Additionally, the older students are more likely to have had parasite-related experiences, which many enjoy sharing with classmates and instructors.

Numerous individuals call me for information about parasitic infections or diseases in their pets, production animals, human patients, or family members. Veterinary clients of the WSVL are the most frequent callers, with questions about disease signs, diagnosis, and control. They also sometimes just want to share an experience or discuss an unusual parasite-related event. Medical doctors or nurses sometimes call for information about cases involving a suspected or already identified parasitic infection, delusions of an infection, or someone who has been to a geographical area where parasites are likely to have been acquired. Also common are calls from people who were urged by their veterinarian, medical doctor, county extension agent, or one of my former students to seek information or advice. The information exchanged on the phone with these callers is frequently basic but sometimes graphic and complex; it is almost always mutually beneficial to the caller, me, and my classroom students, to whom I pass the pertinent stories.

Why Teach?

Most of us who enjoy teaching have a strong passion for our professional specialty and gain satisfaction from interacting with students in the classroom or lab. Additionally gratifying is the positive feedback from students and others who have been "turned on" or have personally benefited from parasite-related information. Negative feedback or suggestions for improvement of course structure, information delivery, or scheduling are also beneficial and appreciated, though not always applied or implemented.

Even now, I sometimes wonder how I arrived at my destination and developed such a strong interest in and passion for teaching. Focusing on parasitology as a professional subject was almost accidental, as was joining the faculty at the University of Wyoming. As I consider the reasons I came to this institution, remained here for so many years, and developed a passion for teaching, several factors are clear: I am fascinated by the parasites and their complexities, most people with whom I communicate about the subject are receptive and equally fascinated, the psychology of the classroom interaction with students is challenging, and there is a parental type of satisfaction involved in getting acquainted and interacting with the high-quality youngsters at our university. Many of the students stay in contact years after graduating and moving to other areas. Many of us consider previous students, especially those who have completed graduate degrees under our guidance, as our "academic sons and daughters." Also gratifying are discussions with veterinary clients, medical professionals, and others who frequently call with questions or unique, interesting stories and experiences they wish to share.

Tales of Teaching Value

The stories I consistently use to illustrate important parasite-related information in the classroom or in person-to-person contact differ somewhat, depending on the target audience. Classroom students with medical, veterinary, or microbiology interests usually benefit from stories with varied implications, whereas medical and veterinary professionals typically want information focused on specific problems, such as pathology, transmission, diagnostics, treatment, or prevention. For practical value, the "tales" most beneficial to the different students can be loosely grouped into four classifications. *Familial,* or family-related, stories are largely medically related but may include examples of parasitism of animals with which family members interact. *Delusional* tales fascinate most people, especially those interested in human medicine, but also many individuals with psychology-related curiosity. *Student*-related stories have been shared with me confidentially or with fellow classmates by students who have taken one of my veterinary or medical parasitology courses, and are effective for transmitting memorable information of the subject. *Miscellaneous* tales have a wide range of instructive value with almost every individual or group of people with any interest in human or animal biology.

Familial Tales

The first example of a *familial* tale involves a teenage male from a city in Montana who developed a worm infection that went undiagnosed for three months or longer. He developed diarrhea that progressively worsened, he became anorectic, and he lost weight, from about 160 to 130 pounds in less than two months. An early examination of a stool sample resulted in identification of *Entamoeba coli*, a nonpathogenic amoeba often found incidentally in people with diarrhea. He was treated for the amoeba with Flagyl, a drug not well tolerated by some patients, and the diarrhea continued to worsen. A diagnostic laboratory technician finally, somewhat accidentally, saw some small, active worms in one of the fresh stool samples. A correct diagnosis was finally achieved, and it was the same facultative roundworm invader that killed the puppy in "Miscellaneous Teaching Tales," to follow. Within three days of treatment with a worm-killing drug, the young man began to regain condition and eventually regained full health in about five months. I was contacted by a veterinarian in north-central Wyoming, who became involved with the case when he was asked questions about the worms by a family member who lived in Wyoming. He was also asked to deworm a family cat that had been adopted by the family member in Wyoming and brought in from the disease site in Montana. The medical staff in Montana suggested that the family cat might have been the source of infection for the teenager. The veterinarian arranged phone contact between the family doctor in Montana and me, during which we exchanged much interesting information. After providing medically pertinent information about the worm, I was informed about the details of the ordeal suffered by the infected boy. During our conversation, the doctor also mentioned that the boy's grandmother, who had died a year before the young man's condition began to deteriorate, had experienced symptoms almost identical to those of her grandson. The elderly woman also had cancer, which was not considered critical or terminal at the time she died, but no autopsy was performed or definitive cause of death identified.

Another *familial* tale took place in the late 1980s. A mother from western Wyoming called me regarding her 6-year-old son, after referral by her local veterinarian. After being treated for the nonpathogenic protozoan *Entamoeba coli* with some herbal products that did not relieve the boy's periodic loose stools, the mother conversed with her local veterinarian. She was originally concerned about the boy's health when she noticed some small, somewhat transparent, wormlike objects in his stool, which led to the original stool examination and diagnosis of the harmless amoeba.

When told that *Entamoeba coli* was not a pathogenic agent, she asked me to perform a diagnostic examination of the boy's stool. In a note submitted with the specimen, she said that the sample contained some of the worms she had seen and been concerned about, which had led to her effort to treat his "infection." Thorough examination of the specimen revealed no parasitic or other potentially harmful creatures. The small "worms" that the mother had been concerned about were undigested, droplet-shaped pieces of citrus fruits, mainly from grapefruit. In a follow-up phone call, she acknowledged that grapefruit and oranges were a large component of what she considered a healthy diet for her family. She was relieved to learn that her son was not a host for parasitic worms or protozoa, but was still puzzled about the cause of his intestinal "problem."

A final *familial* tale revolves around a registered nurse with a 4-year-old daughter and 6-year-old son, living in a small town near the Platte River in Wyoming. The mother called me regarding spontaneous diarrhea in both of her children. Diagnosticians in the medical facility in which she worked told her the problem was almost surely due to the bacterium *Escherichia coli,* some strains of which can cause diarrhea. A week of treatment with antibiotics did not relieve the symptoms, and her children were losing condition. Microscopic examination of fecal samples from the kids, in my lab at WSVL, revealed active forms of *Giardia intestinalis,* an intestinal protozoan frequently found in many humans and almost all other mammal species on earth. Treatment with Flagyl soon firmed the stools of the woman's children.

Exactly one year later, to the week, she informed me that her children had again developed diarrhea and requested another stool exam. It was again giardiasis, it was treated, and the symptoms subsided. A year later, the same pattern was repeated. Coincidentally, she lived next door to the city employee who was responsible for treatment of city water, much or all of which was taken out of the Platte River. The infection in her children coincided with the spring runoff of snow from the mountains, which produces turbulence in streams and rivers, and the resulting flushing of infective parasitic cysts and eggs from the sediment.

The city involved recently installed an expensive, sophisticated ozonation water-purification system that effectively kills most or all infectious parasite eggs and cysts. Before moving from Wyoming to Colorado, the woman informed me that her children had recently been found genetically deficient in ability to produce one of the immunoglobulins, a pertinent factor in a person's ability to develop protective immunity to creatures like *Giardia*.

Delusional Tales

My first example of a *delusional* tale involves a longtime (probably the most senior) practitioner of veterinary medicine in Wyoming, who called to share a story he heard from a medical doctor in their small town in central Wyoming. A middle-aged patient met with the doctor for a routine examination and some information about some worm infections that were troubling her. When asked about the worms, she described the swelling of one or both eyelids, from which she would grasp and pull out stocky, squirming bots, similar to those found under the skin on the backs of cattle. As the stunned doctor sat and stared at her, she asked what he thought the worms might be. After a moment of thought, his response to her was that he thought she was either drunk or crazy.

The second example of a *delusional* tale occurred in 2004, when a medical practitioner called me about a patient of his who was convinced he was infected with a tapeworm in his nose. He had collected a number of flat, segmentlike objects, discharged from both of his nostrils, that resembled tapeworm segments he had read about in a book and had also seen in the feces of some sheep. The specimens were sent to the lab at WSVL, where I examined them with a microscope. They were flat, mucoid "scabs" that frequently form in the external portals of the nose. Identificational features included pollen grains from pine trees and shrubs, nasal hairs, small clusters of epithelial cells from the lining of the nasal ducts, and dust particles. Adult segment-producing tapeworms cannot survive outside of the small intestine or, in one case, the bile duct of an animal host.

The final example of a *delusional* tale took place in 2005, when a medical pathologist submitted a "worm" specimen reportedly extracted from under the skin of a male patient's arm and taken to his family practitioner. The 3-inch-long, slender, coiled "worm" had a delicate, tapered posterior end and a blunt, rounded anterior end that was about twice the diameter of the tail. It very much resembled a canine heartworm, an important, pathogenic roundworm parasite of dogs. After examining the specimen microscopically, it was clear that the "worm" had been built from a common plastic stringlike anchor used to fasten tags to clothing items. Both ends of the "worm" were somewhat darkened, compared to the middle portion of the "body." One end had been heated with flame and the end flap pulled off, causing the tapered shape that resembled a tail. The blunt end was similarly melted, but compressed rather than stretched, resulting in the formation of the enlarged ending.

Student-related Tales

My first *student*-related tale involves self-analysis by lab students. For twenty-nine years, students in Diagnostic Parasitology (a medically related course) were encouraged but not required to perform diagnostic analysis on their personal fecal specimens, or those of a family member or friend, during the final week of class in the teaching lab. Most of the students participated in the practice, and some interesting events resulted. One young man attended almost all sessions of lecture and lab during the semester, but had difficulty staying awake during the 8 a.m. lectures. He always seemed to lack energy and consistently looked and acted tired. He seemed to perk up once during the lecture on giardiasis, where the various effects and symptoms caused by the protozoan were discussed. During the final week's diagnostic examination of his personal fecal specimen, we discovered a *Giardia* infection. The infection was confirmed by his family physician, after which he was treated with Flagyl and rapidly lost the daily fatigue that had plagued him since high school. His lethargy had begun soon after a portion of his intestine had been surgically removed due to damage from a motor vehicle collision.

The second *student*-related tale involves students who have had parasitic infections. Such students frequently don't want to make their maladies public. After discussing giardiasis in the WWAMI medical education class several years ago, one of the students from a city in central Wyoming approached me with his story of experience with *Giardia*. During the final two years in high school, he experienced severe intestinal gas production and noise. He described his embarrassment at having to request, and explain why it was necessary, for him to sit near the door in his classrooms. Finally, during his senior year, his infection was identified, and he was treated and relieved of the problem. He admitted to me that, had the condition not been relieved, he would not have considered attending college, much less medical school.

The third *student*-related tale involves a female student athlete enrolled in Diagnostic Parasitology (a medical course) who analyzed the fecal specimen of her roommate. The roommate had been sick, beginning early the previous fall semester, and progressively became more seriously ill, until she had to drop classes before the end of the school term. Diagnoses by three different doctors in Laramie, Wyoming, ranged through mononucleosis, flu, depression, fibromyalgia, chronic fatigue, and other conditions. Her major symptoms were occasional diarrhea, anorexia, fatigue, dizziness, nausea, and mental depression. When analyzed by her roommate in the teaching parasitology lab, *Giardia* was found in her stool. The diagnosis was confirmed at the Student Health Service on campus, after which she was medicated and immediately began to recover. She was able to reenter school the following fall semester.

Miscellaneous Tales

My first *miscellaneous* tale occurred in the late 1980s, when a veterinarian in central Wyoming called to ask about some white and yellowish "blobs" he saw in the breast muscle of some ducks. The objects were about the size of the head of a wooden match and were numerous in the breasts of several mallards and teal shot by waterfowl hunters in his area. Several of the hunters were clients of the veterinarian, and they were concerned about the risk of eating the birds. We identified the agent as a protozoan, common in the muscles of many animals, each of a different specific identification and host animal. Skunks, which are the main host of the parasite found in these ducks, get infected by eating the muscle cysts and pass the protozoa back to the waterfowl in fecal contamination. The protozoa in ducks are very large compared to the related species in elk, deer, cattle, sheep, and other animals. We have since used duck tissue supplied by this veterinarian for instruction in the Veterinary Parasitology teaching laboratory. When fresh, infected duck tissues are needed, one phone call to the veterinarian is all that is needed. Many other species of the protozoan in ducks can be found in the tissues of mammals, including humans, but are normally so small that they are nearly invisible without a microscope. Some cause serious disease, while others are nearly harmless.

The second *miscellaneous* tale involves butchers in private slaughterhouses in various locations in Wyoming, who send pieces of tissue from antelope, deer, elk, moose, cattle, sheep, and pigs to the parasitology lab at WSVL for identification of "white cysts" almost identical to those in the duck breasts. They reliably are identified as larvae of tapeworms. Most are found in muscle, but some are in liver, brain, lungs, or membranes in the body cavity of the animals. The tapeworm adults live in the small intestines of carnivores that feed on the tissues of the prey animals that have the cysts in their organs. The prey animals develop the tissue cysts from eating vegetation or drinking water contaminated with the tapeworm eggs in the carnivore feces. Rare meat is seldom consumed by students aware of these parasitic worms.

A third *miscellaneous* tale relates to bottom-feeding marine fish that are common menu selections in many restaurants and grocery stores across the United States. Halibut, cod, flounder, and sole have a wide and lucrative market, as do salmon, tuna, and other fish. The bottom feeders are special because of a group of roundworms they share with fish-eating marine mammals, including sea lions, seals, and walruses. The larval stages of the worms live in the tissue of the fish, which acquire the larvae by ingesting eggs from the adult worms in feces from the mammals. The adult worms live in the intestines of the mammals, which must ingest the larvae in raw fish to acquire an infection with the adult worms. If the living larvae are eaten by an unnatural host (human), they somehow know they are not in a "normal" host, are unable to develop to adulthood, and begin to migrate aimlessly into bile duct, pancreatic duct, stomach, large intestine, or appendix, and sometimes perforate the walls of those organs.

The recent rise in popularity of sushi and other menu items made with raw fish, especially fresh fish recently harvested and quickly shipped to inland restaurants and fish markets, has exposed and infected many people to the roundworms in fish. For use in the classroom, frozen halibut, cod, or flounder can be purchased in a grocery store and dissected in a classroom lab. The worms, usually dead from freezing, can be pulled out of the tissue. Fresh fillets containing live worms, allowed to warm to room temperature on a counter, will soon produce active worms about 3 or 4 inches long, which crawl out of the fish and begin to migrate, just as they do in the warm gut of a mammal.

Knowledge of these worms and their habits has enabled students, including me, to simultaneously avoid eating risky fish preparations and to educate innocent bystanders for personal entertainment. After ordering a cooked fish sandwich in a fast-food or other restaurant, if the layers of tissue in the fish patty are separated with a fork, the coiled worms can be pulled out for display. Fellow diners nearly always notice the specimens, especially if they are carefully straightened out and held up for display.

My final *miscellaneous* tale involves a two-month-old Pomeranian puppy from a production kennel that was brought home by the young couple who purchased the animal. The puppy died within four days of purchase and was taken to the WSVL for diagnostic examination. The lethal agent was a worm that normally lives free in soil, without needing a host. When it does infect a host animal, it enters the lining of the small intestine, increases to sometimes large populations, and results in fluid and blood loss, as well as severely retarded digestion and absorption of food. Infected animals and people develop dysenteric, bloody stools, quickly lose body condition, and die—unless diagnosed and treated. The worm causes a dangerous infection in animals and people, and is difficult to identify in a typical infection, because few or no eggs can be found in a stool specimen. Eggs are the primary diagnostic feature in diagnostic tests for intestinal worm infections. An additional, unique ability of this worm is that one of the larval stages of the free-living organism in soil can penetrate the skin of an animal that touches it, migrate through the bloodstream to the intestine, and eventually develop into a parasitic, adult female worm.

In this case, the kennel from which the infected puppy came had been previously cited for violation of public health regulations, because of contamination of their kennel facilities with the worm. The kennel moved to a new location outside of the city limits in which it was cited but apparently did not eliminate the problem from the breeding stock.

Educational (and Practical) Value of 'Tales'

Those of us who enjoy teaching our science specialties get great satisfaction from motivating students to learn as much as possible about our subjects in the short periods of time available to us in the classroom. I am thankful to have been able to inject memorable stories into some of the humdrum instructional terminology, biology, taxonomy, and epidemiology that is a necessary part of "learning the language" of any infectious-disease subject. During the basic scientific information, one or more of the "tales" illustrate to students the applicability of many of the terms, some of which are even difficult to pronounce. When the textbook-level, basic information in the classroom is not being absorbed, "cognitive drift" can be relieved by injection of a true story that is graphic enough to refocus class attention, illustrate the importance of the topic, and stimulate questions or discussion among the students.

Feedback from students through personal contact and written course evaluations consistently confirms my opinion of the instructional value of true stories used in the classroom. I can only guess about the benefit of my interaction with medical practitioners, who call when a puzzling case enters their clinic but seldom provide any feedback regarding the outcome. Their cases do benefit students in the medical education and undergraduate classrooms, where they are used in structured teaching. I feel concern that most practicing medical doctors with whom I have discussed real or delusional parasitic infections in their patients, often have little understanding of such common invaders as worms and protozoa. Pathogenic bacteria and viruses are much more anticipated, quickly diagnosed, and treated than the parasites, which seem to be completely overlooked in many cases, exemplified by several of the tales just told.

Much discussion involving parasitic diseases of animals and humans is exchanged on the phone with veterinarians in Wyoming and other states as distant as Alaska. Preveterinary students benefit from many of those cases, as do the premedical and medical technology students from knowledge about the human infections. In addition, the owners of food-producing or companion animals are provided knowledge that enhances their ability to efficiently and economically maintain the health of their cattle, horses, sheep, dogs, and cats, and enables them to prevent infection of family members with worms and protozoa that can cross the human–domestic-animal fence. The economic benefit of parasite-related knowledge to many ranchers in the United States is consistently estimated in millions of dollars annually; the information that facilitates the financially beneficial control practices is most often provided by a well-educated veterinarian.

12

Steven W. Horn

Steven W. Horn is a professor of animal science at the University of Wyoming. He was appointed dean of the College of Agriculture in 1993 and served in that capacity for eight years before assuming his current position. Professor Horn is a former commissioner of agriculture for the state of Colorado. He began his service in 1978 as a resource conservationist in the Colorado Department of Natural Resources. He served as director of the Colorado State Conservation Board for five years before moving to the Department of Agriculture as deputy commissioner, where he was appointed commissioner of agriculture in 1987. He has served as president of the Western United States Agricultural Trade Association, president of the Western Association of State Departments of Agriculture, and on the board of directors of the National Association of State Departments of Agriculture. As professor of animal science, his current research is directed toward developing orally deliverable compounds to control the rate of reproduction in coyotes and the development of coyote-specific delivery mechanisms for orally activated baits. Professor Horn earned his B.S., M.S., and Ph.D. degrees in the fields of wildlife biology and zoology. He is a U.S. Army veteran who served in Vietnam.

Awakenings

The conversation was strange, one-sided, and seemingly disjointed. It was something about the number of dentine lakes anterior to the top and lingual to the left on the last molar that distinguished the skull of *Microtus ochrogastor* from *pennsylvanicus*, or was it *montanus*. Suddenly, he was quoting Abraham Lincoln, that line about fooling some of the people some of the time….His words faded into the background, swirling lazily toward the ceiling in a gauze of smoke from his nonfiltered Lucky Strike Red. I was standing; he was sitting. Had he invited me to sit, there was no place amid the clutter. I stared at the tiny holes burned through the folds of his white shirt, the cigarette bobbing between his lips. He had shaved, but not well. Confused as to why he had summoned me to his office, my mind raced. Had I been that obvious when peeking at Missy, the beauty pageant queen, during class, her miniskirt not much longer than a vole's tail? Was he so impressed by my taxonomic prowess that he was offering me an assistantship? The realization of why Dr. Bruce "The Meadow Moose," renowned mammalogist, had singled me out from the huge class in the tiered auditorium slowly descended upon me, a heavy, cold accusation of ethical misconduct. I had cheated. Guilty, I proclaimed, hoping for mercy, innocence my defense. I had turned in a museum mount study skin of *Microtus pennsylvanicus* with the skull of *Microtus ochrogaster*, implying they came from the same animal.

A poker game with my cigar-smoking, beer-swilling roommates, followed by the usual slugfest and accordion jam session had distracted me from my lab assignment. Boiling the brains out of the vole's skull in a Dinty Moore Beef Stew can filled the tiny apartment with an aroma not easily forgotten. My roommates fought back with Missouri Crooks, cheap cigars soaked in even cheaper rum. Lyle, a hapless dull normal, scraped the pot to his side of the table and proclaimed a straight flush with only three cards, two diamonds, and a spade. Mickey, the Golden Gloves champ with a short fuse, who delighted in beating us unconscious, quickly produced several pairs of blood-stained boxing gloves. The ensuing carnage claimed the last of the furniture, Bobby the banker's toenail, and my vole skull. No problem, the freezer was filled with voles. Grab one, off with the head, into the can, add water and Clorox, a little stink, and voilà, skin and skull, lab assignment complete. I had trapped the voles in the same meadow and keyed the first one as *pennsylvanicus*. Therefore, they were all *pennsylvanicus*. My A became a B.

Missy the queen and I pulled an all-nighter studying for the big exam that would redeem my character and my grade. I aced it. All right, America!

The following day the Students for a Democratic Society (SDS) attempted to take over the ROTC building in a militant display of antiwar aggression. Finding the doors locked, but with adrenaline spiked and a cause in need of support, the angry crowd went next door and claimed zoology. It took three days for the National Guard to rout them from the barricaded building. Freezers and incubators had been unplugged, research ruined, our tests scattered, drenched in tear gas. A makeup exam by a very angry mammalogy professor was given without warning on our first day back in class. My B became a C.

Seeking solace from Missy the queen, on whom I had spent a fortune trying to impress, she informed me she was engaged. I went back to the apartment and offended Mickey.

After recovery, with graduation in sight, my future ahead of me, I drew a number in the draft lottery that assured an all-expenses-paid vacation to Southeast Asia as soon as my student deferment expired. I found Mickey sleeping peacefully back at the apartment, his high lottery number stenciled on his forehead, a smile on his lips. I poked him with a stick.

In spite of the C grade, a failed relationship, and the certainty of death fighting for an honorable and just peace, something miraculous had happened to me that quarter. It would take years before I understood it, but there had been an awakening.

⊷⊷✦⊷⊷

There is a brief period in our lives that haunts us pleasantly throughout the sum of our experiences, enduring warmly when all else seems cold and chaotic. Often it is the remembrances of our college years that serves as life's benchmark, an eye blink of time against which we measure, judge, and attribute cause. For many, those four short years defined the past and shaped our future. For some of us, it is a single experience with which we associate our chosen path. We crossed that shadowy line into adulthood without realizing we could never go back. But back we go, often when we least expect it. The human mind is an amazing organ, traveling in time in living color and intimate detail, sparking emotion with each remembrance. It allows us to ponder different fates if only we had taken the path less traveled. It allows us to bask in the sentimental glow of a seemingly less complex time, when friends were crazy, loves were innocent, and youthful indiscretions were expected. There were awakenings.

— ⋯✦⋯ —

Scholarly pursuit is often remembered only by the eccentricities of professors and the all-nighters suffered before an exam. Schools had spirit, friends boxed you unconscious, your date wore a tiara, and your mother telegraphed guilt in all correspondence. Few people can explain why we hold our college years so close to our hearts, but college development officers recognized long ago that alumni will give money to preserve those remembrances. The passion of relationships with both people and places during those short four years bubbles to the surface triggered by a song, the smell of pizza, or the sight of a '63 Comet convertible. The nostalgic undertow threatens to pull the unsuspecting alumnus into the murky depths of times remembered.

An education is a complex experience of love, of angst, of hard work, and of sheer joy. It is a journey that we remember for the remainder of our complex lives, a journey that, for the most part, took us to where we are now. The things we learned, the people we met, influenced our choices in life, some more than others, but all beneficial. Most are unaware that it was a shared journey. Shared with friends and family, each with their own remembrances and values associated with those four years. Some of the traveling companions on that short journey were the people who shared their lives in fifty-minute increments, the teachers.

Looking back over the ten-plus years I spent in college, I'm shocked by how few teachers I truly remember. Three courses in statistics, and I cannot remember their names or recall their faces. Ten semester hours of German, and all I remember is that the guy was small in stature, no face, no name, just slight of build. I remember my ichthyology professor from a single thirty-second sound byte in 1967 when he proclaimed that the only thing his generation did wrong was to produce too many of us. I remember my physics professor, soft-spoken with Einstein eyebrows, help-ing me compassionately with the two trains that left the station at the same time.

But I do remember the faculty who *taught* me. Sure, I can figure mean, median, and mode and know the difference between a shark and a wall-eye, but I remember the ones who truly taught me, the teachers who made me want to learn, who illuminated the dark recesses of my mind, the ones who made me ask the how and why questions.

I received a C in the class that most influenced my career, perhaps my life. The professor had caught my ethical indiscretion (cheating). But he had taught me more than the subtleties of academic dishonesty. It was more than his chain-smoking of Luckies in class or the fact that he wore the same clothes—dark slacks, white shirt, and sailor shoes—every day, or his strange inflections whereby mouse became moose and skunk became skoonk. It was an academic awakening. For once everything had purpose, and all the loose ends were tied together. There was meaning in my educa-tion and life. In a general sense, I knew what I wanted to do.

After graduation, Dr. Bruce "The Meadow Moose" removed his own brains with a .38. I never learned why. The speculation was cancer. I sent the obituary to Missy, now a Mrs. She did not respond. The SDS, some believe, burned down Old Main, and I went to Vietnam for a year. But I never forgot the man who inspired my passion for science. Nearly forty years have passed, and I often think of him. I cite his work when possible and sometimes leaf through his book, remembering, still learning.

⊷ ⚌⊹⚌ ⊷

Today in higher education, we spend much time and energy assess-ing student learning, strategizing how to engage critical-thinking skills, developing learning communities, and formulating outcomes, all impor-tant components in education. But formal education generally requires two people for learning to occur: a teacher and a student. This teaching-learning dyad is often overlooked, difficult to measure, and impossible to standardize.

Teachers, as with students, require positive reinforcement. Without it, their teaching behaviors (responses) eventually become extinct. Performance appraisals, pay raises, and student evaluations are part of the complex reinforcement schedule that can help motivate a teacher. Usually there is a temporal component to reinforcement theory that requires rewards (or punishment) to be closely associated in time and space with the response. We often observe such eureka moments in class when learning occurs, eyes widen, heads nod, smiles appear, hands go up. Some students will be bold enough to approach the teacher after class to share a personal experience or ask a question. They have connected the dots, and the picture has emerged. Some, of course, are only concerned about what will be on the next test, passing the course their primary consideration, learning secondary. In humans, however, reinforcement schedules can be very complex, the reward delivered years after the desired behavior.

Teachers invest time, energy, and emotion with their students. We are amused by their freshman naiveté, the world at their feet, so many pieces of candy to choose from. We scowl at their senioritis when they think they have all the answers and the world needs their services, now. We watch them from afar, speculating as to their future and whether we have invested enough in them to someday receive the dividend of a positive memory, someone from whom they learned. Selfish? Perhaps. But learning is not just about the student; neither is it only about the teacher. Learning is about the complex relationship that occurs between the two.

Do fifty students in a tiered classroom negate the possibility of the teacher-student dyad forming? For some, yes. These students will meld into the background, cryptic in every way. Their objective is to not be noticed, to simply be a name on a bubble sheet. They are not the ones to approach the lectern, knock on your door, or flash across your computer screen with an e-mail address that would make their mothers blush. Those students intrigue me. They, too, have a story, and it is often more interesting than the unsolicited confessions that appear after class. The trick is to draw them out, to give them individualized attention. No matter how bad the paper is, a positive comment written above their grade will help in creating that bond. Teach them something that makes them smile with appreciation, something they will remember, something they will associate with you forty years into the future. Who says teaching cannot include memorable experiences, eureka moments? Disciplinary minutia and scientific trivia should not overshadow the big-picture issues that cause students to awaken. Yes, you need the trivia to build suspense, to create conflict, but do not allow it to become the plot. Students are smart. They will connect the dots, and when they do, the picture will be more beautiful than if you had flashed it on the screen for them. That learning moment is a wonderful experience for both the teacher and the student.

Someone once said the future isn't what it used to be. The future of the hopeful freshman and the skeptical senior will be different than they envisioned. Few will spend their lives in the profession they dreamed of. Life often gets in the way. Dreams fade as new visions appear, as new interests develop, as necessity dictates. Forty years from now, will today's student care about DNA sequencing, Bowman's capsule, or the sodium pump? Perhaps not directly. Rather, their education has, hopefully, provided them the ability to appreciate science, the arts, and the humanities, and to ask the right questions by thinking critically. And, when they do, they will remember. They will think again about those different paths, the choices they have made. They will stand back far enough to see themselves as someone they are not, someone they once dreamed of being, or someone they aspire to be. They take comfort in knowing that their education has provided them with the option of traveling back to the future. They will remember their awakenings, not the specifics, but they will associate the event with people, places, and times of their lives. Those will be pleasant memories. Even the unpleasant memories have a way of mellowing with time, sometimes slipping below the conscious and disappearing altogether. We remember the good and forget the bad.

Horror stories abound. Urban legends become reality with time. Students remember or think they remember what they have heard, sometimes what they have seen. They talk with each other about their teachers, passing on what they have been told to believe or expect. Conformity is socially critical. Listen to students talk about their classes and professors. Really listen and you will hear repetitive themes, stories, and the same tidbits of gossip passed down from seniors to freshmen year after year. University professors are remembered as either good or bad, without an intermediate category. Someone who is viewed as "okay" fades easily from their memories within the first decade after graduation. They remember the extremes.

Teachers, too, remember the extremes. The extremes seem to rise to the surface more quickly, pushing other memories aside. It's hard to forget the identical twins who represented each other to avoid penalties for absences. I may never forget the ex-marine who shouted an obscenity having to do with bovine feces when he disagreed with a portion of my lecture. But I also remember the students who smiled with approval as the puzzle was solved or nodded in recognition of a familiar concept. Most remain faceless bodies occupying seats in myriad classrooms. They were in the middle, overshadowed by the extremes.

— ❦ —

Several years ago, I was seated at a banquet table, a crisp white table-cloth covered with a confusing array of silverware and glasses. Seated next to me was an elderly gentleman who thirty-some years earlier had struck fear into my heart. He had been my dean. I had only one experience with the fearsome leader of the college, and it had been extreme. A chronic math phobic, I had gone to him in an attempt to substitute dummy math for trigonometry. Apparently, he was having a bad day, as deans often do, dealing with students trying to weasel their way through the curriculum. He yelled at me, jumped up from behind his desk, and angrily pointed to his office door while threatening my academic career. Shaken, my tail tucked, I slunk back to my apartment to lick my wounds. Later that evening, I experienced an awakening. If I were to attain my career objective, make my parents proud, realize some benefit from my self-sacrifice (living like a vagrant), I would need to change my ways. I would have to buckle down, stop looking for the easy path, set priorities while always remembering why I was there. It had taken a couple of years, but I became a good student, apparently needing someone to yell at me—a parental substitute who scared the living bejesus out of me.

An octogenarian and long retired, the old man had mellowed considerably. We conversed pleasantly, remembering the old days—"Pass the rolls, please." He did not remember me. I was then dean of a college and there to be recognized as the outstanding alumnus of the institution where I had tried to weasel out of trigonometry and had cheated on my mammal-ogy lab assignment. We talked about deanly things. I wanted to tell him, to thank him for scaring me into academic success, but I could not find the courage or the words. He had changed my life and would never know it. But, near the end of the banquet, awards bestowed, thanks given, I realized it was my remembrance, my epiphany, not his. The significance of the event so long ago was insignificant to him. He had his own awakenings. And that is how it should be.

Flattering as it may be to hear from someone whom you influenced, the reality is that you will never hear from most of them again. Like the years, I sometimes wonder where they have gone. If we invoked a positive memory, perhaps someone who helped create an awakening, someone who helped them learn, they will remember. When they solve the problem, grope for the right word, or reach for the book on the shelf, their curiosity piqued by the love of discovery, they will remember. The flood of associated memories will also pour in through that open portal. They will remember the person they sat next to in the class where they experienced an awakening. Suddenly, they hear the roar of the crowd at the game where winning was a surprise; they see the sun shining on a crisp fall day and smell the excitement in the air. They probably will not recall the day or perhaps even the year when learning occurred. They may see flashes of colored chalk, the diagram in the text, or hear the passion in their teacher's voice. But the awakening and all its triggered associations will make their eyes burn and their skin tingle, the corners of their mouth turning upward in recognition of a former time that was happy. The wistful remembrances are all tied together.

A teacher's goal is not to become a part of a student's sentimental yearning for the past. The old professorial mantra of discovering the truth and then teaching it should be the foundation of our motivation. If we do it well, however, they will remember, and if it is sentimental, then so be it. Selfishly accept it as one of the rewards of the profession.

Disappointment, perhaps regret, will sometimes seep into the chemical ooze of recall. Lost opportunities abound. Regretfully I have watched the brightest and the best fade quickly into the murky realm of the forgotten. They were the superstars who made it look so easy. These were the students whom faculty talked about with each other, winking with self-appointed pride, assured of the students' contribution to the future. The students who would replace us. The ones who would go on to greatness in our smug, egotistical interpretation of success. Then life happens. They fall in love with people who are seemingly the most improbable matches; they have babies and then more babies. They stay at home. They become welders and truck drivers and move to obscure places to raise horses, families, and acquire debt. They meld into society. "Tsk, tsk," we say to each other, shaking our heads with disdain as we look down our noses at the path they have chosen, our investment in them wasted. We are unaware that it is our inability to define success that is the true cause of our disappointment.

⊷ ⋈⊹⋈ ⊶

Education cannot be wasted, and it cannot be taken away. Education is forever. Success is a fleeting, abstract phenomenon with so many variables that we tend to oversimplify its definition. The university is not a trade school. Rather, it provides a liberal education, regardless of academic concentration, that allows students to appreciate the world around them. If success can be equated with happiness, then it must be defined by the individual. Academic enlightenment is a lifelong phenomenon no matter what one's occupation. If we taught them critical-thinking skills, our mission has been accomplished. Asking the appropriate questions and knowing how to find the answers should be the true measure of success. Some would argue that education leads to frustration when career goals are not met, that ignorance is bliss. But understanding the difference between ignorance and enlightenment necessitates education.

Students will warmly remember the teachers who helped them to understand. If they believe they have failed to meet your expectations, your memory will fade into the realm of unpleasant experiences. Students are individuals, each one learning differently from the other. Having the same expectations of everyone is unrealistic, but that is what we require. That is how we test, how we measure what they have learned. Our one-size-fits-all approach to assessing student learning employed during midterms and finals yields their grade, but not their learning. What they remember forty years from now may be a truer reflection of how they assimilate knowledge. They will remember the good things. Making learning memorable for the individual, creating the atmosphere for an awakening, is, perhaps, the best measure of student learning.

The author Ann Beattie said, "People forget years and remember moments." A teacher's job is to create those moments. Some refer to them as learning moments, but that seems a short-term oversimplification. Forty years later, they will be threads within the fabric of memory, a patchwork of happy times, of extremes that haunt us pleasantly as our college years. A time when friends were crazy, loves were innocent, and youthful indiscretions were expected. A time of awakenings.

When we least expect it, we take comfort there.